THE OECONOMY OF HUMAN LIFE.

TRANSLATED
From an INDIAN MANUSCRIPT,
written by an Ancient BRAMIN.

To which is prefixed,

An Account of the Manner in which
the said Manuscript was discovered:

IN

A LETTER from an *English* Gentleman, residing in *China*, to the Earl of ****.

IN TWO PARTS.

COVENTRY:
Printed and Sold by M. LUCKMAN.
M DCC LXXVII.

ADVERTISEMENT TO THE PUBLIC.

THE spirit of virtue and morality, which breathes in this ancient piece of eastern instruction, its force and conciseness, and the hopes that it may do good, have prevailed with the person to whom it was sent, to communicate to the public what was translated only for his particular amusement. There are some reasons which at present make it proper to conceal, not only his own name, but the name of his correspondent; who has now resided in *China* several years, and been engaged in a business very different from that of collecting literary curiosities. These reasons will not subsist long; and, as he seems to intimate a design, on his return to *England*, of publishing an entire translation of *Cao-tsou*'s whole journey, the public will then, in all probability, have an opportunity of being satisfied concerning any particulars which they may be curious to know.

CONTENTS
OF
PART I.

PREFACE, - - - - - *page* 9
INTRODUCTION, - - - 21
BOOK I. Duties that relate to MAN considered as an INDIVIDUAL.

1. *Consideration,* - - - - - 23
2. *Modesty,* - - - - - - 25
3. *Application,* - - - - - 27
4. *Emulation,* - - - - - 29
5. *Prudence,* - - - - - - 32
6. *Fortitude,* - - - - - 35
7. *Contentment,* - - - - - 37
8. *Temperance,* - - - - - 39

BOOK II. The PASSIONS.

1. *Hope and fear,* - - - - 44
2. *Joy and grief,* - - - - 46
3. *Anger,* - - - - - - 49
4. *Pity,* - - - - - - 52
5. *Desire and love,* - - - - 54

A 3   BOOK

BOOK III. WOMAN, 56

BOOK IV. Consanguinity, or Natural Relations.

1. Husband, - - - - - - - 60
2. Father, - - - - - - - 62
3. Son, - - - - - - - - 64
4. Brothers, - - - - - - 66

BOOK V. Providence; or, The accidental Differences of Men.

1. Wise and ignorant, - - - - 67
2. Rich and poor, - - - - - 69
3. Masters and servants, - - - 73
4. Magistrates and subjects, - - 74

BOOK VI. The Social Duties.

1. Benevolence, - - - - - - 79
2. Justice, - - - - - - - 81
3. Charity, - - - - - - - 83
4. Gratitude, - - - - - - 84
5. Sincerity, - - - - - - 86

CONTENTS.

BOOK VII. RELIGION. 89

CONTENTS of PART II.

BOOK I. Man considered in the general.

1. *Of the human frame and structure,* 99
2. *Of the use of the senses,* - - - 102
3. *The soul of man, &c.* - - - 105
4. *Of the period and uses of human life,* 111

BOOK II. Man considered in regard to his Infirmities, and their Effects.

1. *Vanity,* - - - - - - 118
2. *Inconstancy,* - - - - - - 122
3. *Weakness,* - - - - - - 128
4. *Of the insufficiency of knowledge,* 133
5. *Misery,* - - - - - - 139
6. *Of Judgment,* - - - - - 143
7. *Presumption,* - - - - - 149

CONTENTS.

BOOK III. Of the Affections of Man which are hurtful to himself and others.

1. *Covetousness,* - - - - - 155
2. *Profusion,* - - - - - - 159
3. *Revenge,* - - - - - - 161
4. *Cruelty, hatred, and envy,* - 166
5. *Heaviness of heart,* - - - 171

BOOK IV. Of the Advantages Man may acquire over his fellow Creatures.

1. *Nobility and honour,* - - - 178
2. *Science and learning,* - - - 184

BOOK V. Of Natural Accidents.

1. *Prosperity and adversity,* - - 188
2. *Pain and sickness,* - - - - 192
3. *Death,* - - - - - - - 194

TO THE

Earl of ------.

Peking, May 12, 1749.

My Lord,

IN the laſt Letter which I had the honour of writing to your Lordſhip, dated *Dec.* 23d, 1748, I think I concluded all I had to ſay, in regard to the topography and natural hiſtory of this great empire. I purpoſed in this, and ſome ſucceeding ones, to have ſet down ſuch obſervations, as I have been able to make on the laws, government, religion, and manners of the people. But a remarkable occurrence has happened lately, which ingroſſes the converſation of the *literati* here; and may here-

hereafter, perhaps, afford matter of speculation to the learned in *Europe*. As it is of a nature which, I know, will furnish some entertainment to your Lordship, I will endeavour to give you as distinct and particular an account of it, as I have been able to obtain.

Adjoining to *China* on the *West*, is the large country of *Thibet*, called by some *Barantola*. In a province of this country, named *Lasa*, resides the grand Lama, or high-priest, of these idolaters; who is reverenced, and even adored as a God, by most of the neighbouring nations. The high opinion which is entertained of his sacred character, induces prodigious numbers of religious people to resort to *Lasa*, to pay their homage to him, and to give him presents in order to receive his blessing. His residence is in a most magnificent pagod, or temple, built on the top of the mountain *Poutala*. The foot of this mountain, and even the whole district of *Lasa*, is inhabited by an incredible num-

number of Lamas of different ranks and orders, several of whom have very grand pagods erected to their honour, in which they receive a kind of inferior worship. The whole country, like *Italy*, abounds with priests; and they entirely subsist on the great number of rich presents, which are sent them from the utmost extent of *Tartary*, from the empire of the *Great Mogul*, and from almost all parts of the *Indies*. When the grand Lama receives the adorations of the people, he is raised on a magnificent altar, and sits cross-legg'd, upon a splendid cushion: his worshippers prostrate themselves before him in the humblest and most abject manner; but he returns not the least sign of respect, nor ever speaks, even to the greatest princes; he only lays his hand upon their heads, and they are fully persuaded, that they receive from thence a full forgiveness of all their sins. They are likewise so extravagant as to imagine, that he knows all things, even the secrets of the heart;

and

and his particular disciples being a select number of about two hundred of the most eminent Lamas, have the address to make the people believe he is immortal; and that, whenever he appears to die, he only changes his abode, and animates a new body.

The learned in *China* have long been of opinion, that, in the archives of this grand temple, some very ancient books have for many ages been concealed: and the present emperor, who is very curious in searching after the writings of antiquity, became at length so fully convinced of the probability of this opinion, that he determined to try whether any discovery of this sort could be made. To this end, his first care was to find out a person eminently skilful in the ancient languages and characters. He at length pitch'd upon one of the *Hanlins*, or doctors of the first order, whose name was *Cao-tsou*, a man about fifty years of age, of a grave and noble aspect, of great eloquence, and who, by

an

an accidental friendship with a certain learned Lama, who had resided many years at *Peking*, was become entirely master of the language which the Lamas of *Thibet* use among themselves.

With these qualifications he set forward on his journey; and, to give his commission the greater weight, the Emperor honour'd him with the title of *Colao*, or prime minister: to which he added a most magnificent equipage and attendants; with presents for the grand Lama, and the other principal Lamas, of an immense value; also a letter written with his own hand, in the following terms.

To the Great

Representative of GOD.

Most High, most Holy, and Worthy to be adored!

" WE, the Emperor of *China*, So-
" vereign of all the Sovereigns
" of the earth, in the person of this our
" most

"most respected Prime Minister *Cao-tsou*, with all reverence and humility prostrate ourself beneath thy sacred feet, and implore for ourself, our friends, and our empire, thy most powerful and gracious benediction.

"Having a strong desire to search into the records of antiquity, to learn and retrieve the wisdom of the ages that are past: and being well informed, that in the sacred repositories of thy most ancient and venerable hierarchy, there are some valuable books, which, from their great antiquity, are become to the generality even of the learned, almost wholly unintelligible; in order, as far as in us lies, to prevent their being totally lost, we have thought proper to authorise and employ our most learned and respected Minister *Cao-tsou*, in this our present embassy to thy Sublime Holiness; the business of which is to desire, that he may be permitted to read and examine the said writings;

"ings; we expecting, from his great
"and uncommon skill in the ancient
"languages, that he will be able to in-
"terpret whatever may be found, tho'
"of the highest and most obscure an-
"tiquity. And we have commanded
"him to throw himself at thy feet,
"with such testimonies of our respect,
"as, we trust, will procure him the
"admittance we desire."

I will not detain your Lordship with any particulars of his journey, tho' he hath published a large account of it, abounding with many surprising relations; and which, at my return to *England*, I may probably translate and publish intire. Let it suffice at present, that, when he arrived in these sacred territories, the magnificence of his appearance, and the richness of his present, failed not to gain him a ready admission. He had apartments appointed him in the sacred college, and was assisted in his inquiries by one of the most

most learned Lamas. He continued there near six months: during which time he had the satisfaction of finding many valuable pieces of antiquity; from some of which he hath made very curious extracts, and hath formed such probable conjectures concerning their authors, and the times wherein they were written, as proves him to be a man of great judgment and penetration, as well as most extensive reading.

But the most ancient piece he hath discovered, and which none of the Lamas for many ages had been able to interpret or understand, is a small system of morality, written in the language and character of the ancient Gymnosophists or Bramins; but by what particular person, or in what time, he does not pretend to determine. This piece, however, he wholly translated; though, as he himself confesses, with an utter incapacity of reaching, in the

Chinese

Chinese language, the strength and sublimity of the original. The judgments and opinions of the Bonzees, and the learned Doctors, are very much divided concerning it. Those who admire it most highly, are very fond of attributing it to *Confucius*, their own great philosopher; and get over the difficulty of its being written in the language and character of the ancient Bramins, by supposing this to be only a translation, and that the original work of *Confucius*, is lost. Some will have it to be the institutes of *Lao Kiun*, another *Chinese* philosopher, cotemporary with *Confucius*, and founder of the sect *Tao-ssée*; but these labour under the same difficulty, in regard to the language, with those who attribute it to *Confucius*. There are others, who from some particular marks and sentiments which they find in it, suppose it to be written by the Bramin *Dandamis*, whose famous letter to *Alexander* the Great is recorded by the *European* writers. With these *Cao-tsou* himself seems most inclined to agree; at least so far as to think, that it is really the work of some ancient Bramin; being fully persuaded, from the spirit with which it is written, that it is no translation. One thing however, occasions some doubt amongst them, and that is the plan of it; which is entirely new to the Eastern people, and so unlike any thing they have ever seen, that, if it was not for some turns of expression peculiar to the East, and the impossibility of accounting for its being written in this very ancient language, many would suppose it to be the work of an *European*.

But whoever was the writer of it, the great noise which it makes in this city, and all over the empire, the eagerness with which it is read by all kinds of people, and the high encomiums which are given to it by some, at length de-

determined me to attempt a translation of it into *English*; especially as I was persuaded, it would be an agreeable present to your Lordship. And I was the more easily induced to make this trial, as, very happily for me, you cannot judge how far I have fallen short of the original, or even of the *Chinese* translation. One thing, however, it may perhaps be necessary to apologize for, at least to give some account of; and that is, the style and manner in which I have translated it. I can assure your Lordship, that when I first sat down to the work, I had not the least intention of doing it in this way; but the sublime manner of thinking which appeared in the Introduction, the great energy of expression, and the shortness of the sentences, naturally led me into this kind of style: and I hope, the having so elegant a pattern to form myself upon, as our version of the book of *Job*, the *Psalms*, the works of *So-*
lomon,

xx The OECONOMY, &c. Pref.

lomon, and the Prophets, hath been of some advantage to my translation.

Such as it is, if it affords your Lordship any entertainment, I shall think myself extremely happy; and in my next will resume my account of this people and their empire.

I am, &c.

INTRODUCTION.

BOW down your heads unto the dust, O ye inhabitants of earth! be silent, and receive with reverence, instruction from on high.

Wheresoever the sun doth shine, wheresoever the wind doth blow, wheresoever there is an ear to hear, and a mind to conceive; there let the precepts of life be made known, let the maxims of truth be honour'd and obey'd.

All things proceed from God. His power is unbounded, his wisdom is from eternity; and his goodness endureth for ever.

He sitteth on his throne in the centre, and the breath of his mouth giveth life to the world.

He toucheth the stars with his finger, and they run their course rejoicing.

On the wings of the wind he walketh abroad, and performeth his will thro' all the regions of unlimited space.

Order, and grace, and beauty, spring from his hand.

The voice of wisdom speaketh in all his works; but the human understanding comprehendeth it not.

The shadow of knowledge passeth over the mind of man as a dream: he seeth as in the dark; he reasoneth and is deceived.

But the wisdom of God is as the light of heaven: he reasoneth not; his mind is the fountain of truth.

Justice and mercy wait before his throne; benevolence and love enlighten his countenance for ever.

Who is like unto the Lord in glory? who in power shall contend with the Almighty? hath he any equal in wisdom? can any goodness be compared unto him?

He it is, O man, who hath created thee; thy station on earth is fixed by his appointment: the powers of thy mind are the gifts of his goodness; the wonders of thy frame are the work of his hand.

Hear then his voice, for it is gracious; and he that obeyeth, shall establish his soul in peace.

BOOK

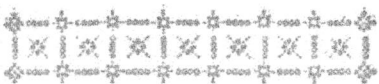

BOOK I.

DUTIES that relate to MAN, considered as an INDIVIDUAL.

CHAP. I.
CONSIDERATION.

COMMUNE with thyself, O man; and consider wherefore thou wert made.

Contemplate thy powers, contemplate thy wants and thy connections; so shalt thou discover the duties of life, and be directed in all thy ways.

Proceed not to speak or to act, before thou hast weighed thy words, and examined the tendency of every step thou shalt take: so shall disgrace fly far from thee,

24 The OECONOMY Part I.

thee, and in thy house shall shame be a stranger; repentance shall not visit thee, nor sorrow dwell upon thy cheek.

The thoughtless man bridleth not his tongue; he speaketh at random, and is entangled in the foolishness of his own words.

As one that runneth in haste, and leapeth over a fence, may fall into a pit which he doth not see; so is the man that plungeth suddenly into any action, before he hath considered the consequences thereof.

Hearken therefore unto the voice of Consideration; her words are the words of wisdom; and her paths shall lead thee to safety and truth.

CHAP.

CHAP. II.
MODESTY.

WHO art thou, O man, that presumest on thine own wisdom? or why dost thou vaunt thyself on thine own acquirements?

The first step towards being wise, is to know that thou art ignorant; and if thou wouldst be esteemed in the judgment of others, cast off the folly of seeming wise in thine own conceit.

As a plain garment best adorneth a beautiful woman, so a decent behaviour is the greatest ornament of wisdom.

The speech of a modest man giveth lustre to truth; and the diffidence of his words excuseth his error.

He relieth not on his own wisdom; he weigheth the counsels of a friend, and receiveth the benefit thereof.

He turneth away his ear from his own praise, and believeth it not: he is the last in discovering his own perfections.

Yet,

Yet, as a veil addeth to beauty, so are his virtues set off by the shade which his modesty casteth upon them.

But behold the vain man, and observe the arrogant: he cloatheth himself in rich attire, he walketh in the public street, he casteth round his eyes, and courteth observation.

He tosseth up his head, and overlooketh the poor; he treateth his inferiors with insolence, and his superiors in return look down on his pride and folly with laughter.

He despiseth the judgment of others; he relieth on his own opinion, and is confounded.

He is puffed up with the vanity of his imagination; his delight is to hear and to speak of himself all the day long.

He swalloweth with greediness his own praise; and the flatterer in return eateth him up.

CHAP. III.
APPLICATION.

SINCE the days that are past are gone for ever, and those that are to come may not come to thee; it behoveth thee, O man, to employ the present time, without regretting the loss of that which is past, or too much depending on that which is to come.

This instant is thine; the next is in the womb of futurity, and thou knowest not what it may bring forth.

Whatsoever thou resolvest to do, do it quickly: defer not till the evening what the morning may accomplish.

Idleness is the parent of want and of pain; but the labour of virtue bringeth forth pleasure.

The hand of diligence defeateth want; prosperity and success are the industrious man's attendants.

Who is he that hath acquired wealth, that hath risen to power, that hath cloathed himself with honour, that is spoken of in the city with praise, and that standeth before the king in his counsel? even he that hath shut out Idleness from his house; and hath said unto Sloth, Thou art mine enemy.

He riseth up early, and lieth down late; he exerciseth his mind with contemplation, and his body with action; and preserveth the health of both.

The slothful man is a burden to himself; his hours hang heavy on his head; he loitereth about; and knoweth not what he would do.

His days pass away like the shadow of a cloud; and he leaveth behind him no mark for remembrance.

His body is diseased for want of exercise; he wisheth for action, but hath not power to move. His mind is in darkness: his thoughts are confused: he longeth for knowledge, but hath no appli-

application. He would eat of the almond, but hateth the trouble of breaking the shell.

His house is in disorder; his servants are wasteful and riotous; and he runneth on towards ruin: he seeth it with his eyes: he heareth it with his ears; he shaketh his head, and wisheth; but hath no resolution: till ruin cometh upon him like a whirlwind; and shame and repentance descend with him to the grave.

CHAP. IV.
EMULATION.

IF thy soul thirsteth for honour, if thy ear hath any pleasure in the voice of praise, raise thyself from the dust whereof thou art made, and exalt thy aim to something that is praiseworthy.

The oak that now spreadeth its branches towards the heavens, was once

once but an acron in the bowels of the earth.

Endeavour to be first in thy calling, whatever it be; neither let any one go before thee in well-doing: nevertheless, do not envy the merits of another, but improve thine own talents.

Scorn also to depress thy competitor by dishonest or unworthy methods; strive to raise thyself above him only by excelling him: so shall thy contest for superiority be crowned with honour, if not with success.

By a virtuous emulation the spirit of man is exalted within him; he panteth after fame, and rejoiceth as a racer to run his course.

He riseth like the palm-tree in spite of oppression: and, as an eagle in the firmament of heaven, he soareth aloft, and fixeth his eye upon the glories of the sun.

The examples of eminent men are in his visions by night; and his delight is to follow them all the day long.

Part I. of HUMAN LIFE.

He formeth great designs; he rejoiceth in the execution thereof; and his name goeth forth to the ends of the world.

But the heart of the envious man is gall and bitterness; his tongue spitteth venom; the success of his neighbour breaketh his rest.

He sitteth in his cell repining; and the good that happeneth to another, is to him an evil.

Hatred and malice feed upon his heart; and there is no rest in him.

He feeleth in his own breast no love of goodness; and therefore believeth his neighbour is like unto himself.

He endeavours to depreciate those who excel him; and putteth an evil interpretation on all their doings.

He lieth on the watch, and meditates mischief: but the detestation of man pursueth him; he is crushed as a spider in his own web.

CHAP. V.
PRUDENCE.

HEAR the words of Prudence; give heed unto her counsels, and store them in thine heart. Her maxims are universal, and all the Virtues lean upon her; she is the guide, and the mistress of human life.

Put a bridle on thy tongue; set a guide before thy lips; lest the words of thine own mouth destroy thy peace.

Let him that scoffeth at the lame, take care that he halt not himself; whosoever speaketh of another's failings with pleasure, shall hear of his own with shame.

Of much speaking cometh repentance; but in silence is safety.

A talkative man is a nuisance to society; the ear is sick of his babbling; the torrent of his words overwhelmeth conversation.

Boast

Boast not of thyself, for it shall bring contempt upon thee; neither deride another, for it is dangerous.

A bitter jest is the poison of friendship; and he who restrains not his tongue, shall live in trouble.

Furnish thyself with the accommodations proper to thy condition; yet spend not to the utmost of what thou canst afford, that the providence of thy youth may be a comfort to thy old age.

Avarice is the parent of evil deeds; but frugality is the sure guardian of our virtues.

Let thine own business engage thy attention; leave the care of the state to the governors thereof.

Let not thy recreations be expensive; lest the pain of purchasing them exceed the pleasure thou hast in their enjoyment.

Neither let prosperity put out the eyes of circumspection, nor abundance cut off the hands of frugality: he that too much indulgeth in the superfluities of life, shall live to lament the want of its necessaries.

Trust no man, before thou hast tried him: yet mistrust not without reason; it is uncharitable.

But when thou hast proved a man to be honest, lock him up in thine heart as a treasure; regard him as a jewel of inestimable price.

Receive not the favours of a mercenary man; nor join in friendship with the wicked; they shall be snares unto thy virtue, and bring grief to thy soul.

Use not to-day, what to-morrow may want; neither leave that to hazard, which foresight may provide for, or care prevent.

From the experience of others do thou learn wisdom; and from their failings correct thine own faults.

Yet expect not even from prudence infallible success; for the day knoweth not what the night may bring forth.

The fool is not always unfortunate, nor the wise man always successful:

yet never had a fool a thorough enjoyment, never was a wise man wholly unhappy.

CHAP. VI.
FORTITUDE.

PERILS, and misfortunes, and want, and pain, and injury, are the lot of every man who cometh into the world.

It behoveth thee, therefore, early to fortify thy mind with courage and patience; that thou mayest support with resolution thy allotted portion of calamity.

As the camel beareth labour, and heat, and hunger, and thirst, through desarts of sand, and fainteth not: so a man of fortitude shall sustain his virtue through perils, and distress.

A noble spirit disdaineth the malice of fortune: his greatness of soul is not to be cast down.

His happiness dependeth not on her smiles, and therefore with her frowns he shall not be dismayed.

As a rock in the sea he standeth firm, and the dashing of the waves disturbeth him not.

He raiseth his head like a tower on an hill; and the arrows of fortune drop at his feet.

In the instant of danger, the courage of his heart sustaineth him; and the steadiness of his mind beareth him out.

He meeteth the evils of life as a man that goeth forth unto battle, and returneth with victory in his hand.

Under the pressure of misfortunes, his calmness alleviates their weight; and by his constancy he shall surmount them.

But the dastardly spirit of a timorous man betrayeth him to shame.

By shrinking under poverty, he stoopeth down to meanness; and by tamely bearing insults, he inviteth injuries.

As a reed is shaken with the breath of the air, so the shadow of evil maketh him tremble.

In the hour of danger, he is embarrassed and confounded; in the day of misfortune he sinketh, and despair overwhelmeth his soul.

CHAP. VII.
CONTENTMENT.

FORGET not, O man, that thy station on earth is appointed by the wisdom of the Eternal; who knoweth thy heart; who seeth the vanity of all thy wishes; and who often in mercy denieth thy requests.

Yet for all reasonable desires, for all honest endeavours, his benevolence hath established, in the nature of things, a probability of success.

The uneasiness thou feelest, the misfortunes thou bewailest; hold the root from whence they spring, even thine own folly, thine own pride, thine own distempered fancy.

Murmur not therefore at the dispensations of God; but correct thine own heart;

heart; neither say within thyself, If I had wealth, power, or leisure, I should be happy; for know, they all bring to their several possessors their peculiar inconveniencies.

The poor man seeth not the vexations and anxieties of the rich; he feeleth not the difficulties and perplexities of power; neither knoweth he the wearisomeness of leisure; and therefore it is that he repineth at his own lot.

But envy not the appearance of happiness in any man; for thou knowest not his secret griefs.

To be satisfied with a little, is the greatest wisdom; and he who increaseth his riches, increaseth his cares; but a contented mind is a hidden treasure, and a guard from trouble.

Yet, if thou sufferest not the blandishments of thy fortunes to rob thee of justice, or temperance, or charity, or modesty, even riches themselves shall not make thee unhappy.

But hence shalt thou learn, that the cup

cup of felicity, pure and unmixed, is by no means a draught for mortal man.

Virtue is the race which God hath set him to run, and happiness the goal; which none can arrive at, till he hath finished his course, and received his crown in the mansions of eternity.

CHAP. VIII.
TEMPERANCE.

THE nearest approach thou canst make to happiness on this side the grave, is to enjoy from heaven health, wisdom, and peace of mind.

These blessings if thou possessest, and wouldst preserve to old age, avoid the allurements of *Voluptuousness*, and fly from her temptations.

When she spreadeth her delicacies on the board, when her wine sparkleth in the cup, when she smileth upon thee, and persuadeth thee to be joyful and happy; then is the hour of danger, then let reason stand firmly on her guard.

For, if thou hearkenest unto the words of her adversary, thou art deceiv'd, and betray'd.

The joy which she promiseth, changeth to madness; and her enjoyments lead on to diseases and death.

Look round her board, cast thine eyes upon her guests, and observe those who have been allured by her smiles, who have listened to her temptations.

Are they not meagre? are they not sickly? are they not spiritless?

Their short hours of jollity and riot are followed by tedious days of pain and dejection; she hath debauch'd and pall'd their appetites, that they have now no relish for her nicest dainties: her votaries are become her victims; the just and natural consequence which God hath ordain'd, in the constitution of things, for the punishment of those who abuse his gifts.

But who is she, that with graceful steps, and with a lively air, trips over yonder plain?

Part I.   of HUMAN LIFE.   41

The rose blusheth on her cheeks; the sweetness of the morning breatheth from her lips; joy, tempered with innocence and modesty, sparkleth in her eyes; and from the chearfulness of her heart, she singeth as she walks.

Her name is Health; she is the daughter of Exercise, who begot her upon Temperance: their sons inhabit the mountains that stretch over the northern regions of *San Ton Hoe*.

They are brave, active, and lively; and partake of all the beauties and virtues of their sister.

Vigour stringeth their nerves; strength dwelleth in their bones: and labour is their delight all the day long.

The employments of their father excite their appetites, and the repasts of their mother refresh them.

To combat the passions, is their delight; to conquer evil habits, their glory.

Their pleasures are moderate, and therefore they endure; their repose is short, but sound and undisturbed.

Their

Their blood is pure, their minds are serene; and the physician knoweth not the way to their habitations.

But safety dwelleth not with the sons of men, neither is security found within their gates.

Behold them exposed to new dangers from without, while a traitor within lurketh to betray them.

Their health, their strength, their beauty and activity, have raised desire in the bosom of *lascivious Love*.

She standeth in her bower, she courteth their regard, she spreadeth her temptations.

Her limbs are soft, her air is delicate, her attire is loose: Wantonness speaketh in her eyes, and on her bosom sits Temptation: she beckoneth them with her finger; she wooeth them with her looks; and by the smoothness of her tongue she endeavoureth to deceive.

Ah! fly from her allurements; stop thine ears to her enchanting words. If thou meetest the languishing of her eyes, if thou hearest the softness of her voice, if she casteth her arms about thee, she bindeth thee in chains for ever.

Shame followeth, and disease, and want, and care, and repentance.

Enfeebled by Dalliance, with Luxury pamper'd, and softened by Sloth, strength shall forsake thy limbs, and health thy constitution; thy days shall be few, and those inglorious; thy griefs shall be many, yet meet with no compassion.

BOOK II.

The PASSIONS.

CHAP. I.

HOPE and FEAR.

THE promises of Hope, are sweeter than roses in the bud, and far more flattering to expectation; but the threatenings of Fear are a terror to the heart.

Nevertheless, let not Hope allure, nor Fear deter thee from doing that which is right; so shalt thou be prepared to meet all events with an equal mind.

The terrors of death are no terrors to the good: restrain thy hand from evil, and thy soul shall have nothing to fear.

In all thy undertakings let a reasonable assurance animate thy endeavours;

if thou despairest of success, thou shalt not succeed.

Terrify not thy soul with vain fears; neither let thy heart sink within thee from the phantoms of imagination.

From Fear proceedeth misfortune; but he that hopeth, helpeth himself.

As the ostrich when pursued hideth his head, but forgetteth his body; so the fears of a coward expose him to danger.

If thou believest a thing impossible, thy despondency shall make it so; but he that persevereth, shall overcome all difficulties.

A vain Hope flattereth the heart of a fool; but he that is wise, pursueth it not.

In all thy desires let reason go before thee; and fix not thy Hopes beyond the bounds of probability; so shall success attend thy undertakings, and thy heart shall not be vexed with disappointments.

CHAP.

CHAP. II.
JOY and GRIEF.

LET not thy mirth be so extravagant as to intoxicate thy mind; nor thy sorrow so heavy, as to depress thy heart: this world affordeth no good so transporting, nor inflicteth any evil so severe, as should raise thee far above, or sink thee much beneath, the balance of moderation.

Lo! yonder standeth the house of *Joy*; it is painted on the outside, and looketh gay; thou mayst know it by the noise of mirth and exultation that issueth from it.

The mistress standeth at the door, and calleth aloud to all that pass by: she singeth, and shouteth, and laugheth without ceasing.

She inviteth them to taste the pleasures of life; which, she telleth them, are no where to be found but beneath her roof.

But enter not thou into her gate; neither associate thyself with those who frequent her house.

They call themselves the sons of *Joy*, they laugh and seem delighted; but madness and folly are in all their doings.

They are link'd with mischief hand in hand, and their steps lead down to evil; dangers beset them round about, and the pit of destruction yawneth beneath their feet.

Look now on the other side; and behold in that vale overshadow'd with trees, and hid from the sight of men, the habitation of *Sorrow*.

Her bosom heaveth with sighs; her mouth is filled with lamentation; she delighteth to dwell on the subject of human misery.

She looketh on the common accidents of life, and weepeth: the weakness and wickedness of man is the theme of her lips.

All nature to her teemeth with evil; every object she seeth, is ting'd with the gloom of her own mind; and the voice of complaint saddeneth her dwelling day and night.

Come not near her cell; her breath is contagious: she will blast the fruits, and wither the flowers, that adorn and sweeten the garden of life.

In avoiding the house of *Joy*, let not thy feet betray thee to the borders of this dismal mansion; but pursue with care the middle path, which shall lead thee by a gentle assent to the bower of *Contentment*.

With her dwelleth peace; with her dwell safety and tranquility. She is chearful, but not gay; she is serious, but not grave; she vieweth the joys and the sorrows of life with steadiness and serenity.

From hence, as from an eminence shalt thou behold the folly and the misery of those, who either, led by the gaiety

gaiety of their hearts, take up their abode with the companions of jollity and riotous mirth; or, infected by gloominess and melancholy, spend all their days in complaining of the woes and calamities of human life.

Thou shalt view them both with pity; and the error of their ways shall keep thy feet from straying.

CHAP. III.

ANGER.

AS the whirlwind in its fury teareth up trees, and deformeth the face of nature, or as an earthquake in its convulsions overturneth cities: so the rage of an angry man throweth mischief around him: danger and destruction wait on his hand.

But consider, and forget not, thine own weakness; so shalt thou pardon the failings of others.

Indulge not thyself in the passion of Anger; it is whetting a sword to wound thy own breast, or murder thy friend.

If thou bearest slight provocations with patience, it shall be imputed unto thee for wisdom; and if thou wipest them from thy remembrance, thy heart shall feel rest, thy mind shall not reproach thee.

Seest thou not, that the angry man loseth his understanding? Whilst thou are yet in thy senses, let the madness of another be a lesson to thyself.

Do nothing in thy passion; why wilt thou put to sea in the voilence of a storm?

If it be difficult to rule thine anger, it is wise to prevent it: avoid therefore all occasions of falling into wrath; or guard thyself against them, whenever they occur.

A fool is provoked with insolent speeches; but a wise man laugheth them to scorn.

Hat-

Harbour not revenge in thy breast; it will torment thy heart, and discolour its best inclinations.

Be always more ready to forgive, than to return an injury: he that watches for an opportunity of revenge, lies in wait against himself, and draweth down mischief on his own head.

A mild answer to an angry man, like water cast upon the fire, abateth his heat; and from an enemy he shall become thy friend.

Consider how few things are worthy of Anger; and thou wilt wonder, that any but fools should be wroth.

In folly or weakness it always beginneth; but remember, and be well assured, it seldom concludeth without repentance.

On the heels of Folly treadeth Shame; at the back of Anger standeth Remorse.

CHAP. IV.
PITY.

AS blossoms and flowers are strewed upon the earth by the hand of Spring, as the kindness of Summer produceth in perfection the bounties of Harvest; so the smiles of Pity shed blessings on the children of Misfortune.

He who pitieth another, recommendeth himself; but he who is without compassion, deserveth it not.

The butcher relenteth not at the bleating of the lamb; neither is the heart of the cruel moved with distress.

But the tears of the compassionate are sweeter than dew-drops falling from roses on the bosom of the earth.

Shut not thine ear therefore against the cries of the poor; neither harden thine heart against the calamities of the innocent.

When

When the Fatherless call upon thee, when the widow's heart is sunk, and she imploreth thy assistance with tears of sorrow; O pity her affliction, and extend thy hand to those who have none to help them.

When thou seest the naked wanderer of the street shivering with cold, and destitute of habitation, let bounty open thine heart; let the wings of charity shelter him from death, that thine own soul may live.

Whilst the poor man groaneth on the bed of sickness, whilst the unfortunate languish in the horrors of a dungeon, or the hoary head of age lifts up a feeble eye to thee for pity; O how canst thou riot in superfluous enjoyments, regardless of their wants, unfeeling of their woes.

CHAP. V.

DESIRE and LOVE.

BEWARE, young man, beware the allurements of *Wantonness*; and let not the harlot tempt thee to her delights.

The madness of desire shall defeat its own pursuits; from the blindness of its rage thou shalt rush upon destruction.

Therefore give not up thy heart to her sweet enticements; neither suffer thy soul to be enslaved by her enchanting delusions.

The fountain of health, which must supply the stream of pleasure, shall quickly be dried up; and every spring of joy shall be exhausted.

In the prime of thy life old age shall overtake thee; thy sun shall decline in the morning of thy days.

But when virtue and modesty enlighten her charms, the lustre of a
beau-

Part I.   of HUMAN LIFE.   55

beautiful woman is brighter than the stars of heaven; and the influence of her power it is in vain to resist.

The whiteness of her bosom transcendeth the lily; her smile is more delicious than a garden of roses.

The innocence of her eye is like that of the turtle; simplicity and truth dwell in her heart.

The kisses of her mouth are sweeter than honey; the perfumes of *Arabia* breathe from her lips.

Shut not thy bosom to the tenderness of Love; the purity of its flame shall ennoble thine heart, and soften it to receive the fairest impressions.

BOOK III.

WOMAN.

GIVE ear, fair daughter of love, to the instructions of Prudence; and let the precepts of truth sink deep in thine heart: so shall the charms of thy mind add lustre to thy form; and thy beauty, like the rose it resembleth, shall retain its sweetness, when its bloom is withered.

In the spring of thy youth, in the morning of thy days, when the eyes of men gaze on thee with delight; ah! hear with caution their alluring words; guard well thy heart, nor listen to their soft seducements.

Remember, thou art made man's reasonable companion, not the slave of his passion; the end of thy being is to assist him in the toils of life, to sooth him with thy tenderness, and recompense his care with soft endearments.

Who is she that winneth the heart of man, that subdueth him to love, and reigneth in his breast?

Lo! yonder she walketh in maiden sweetness, with innocence in her mind, and modesty on her cheek.

Her hand seeketh employment; her foot delighteth not in gadding abroad.

She is cloathed with neatness; she is fed with temperance; humility and meekness are as a crown of glory circling her head.

On her tongue dwelleth music; the sweetness of honey floweth from her lips.

Decency is in all her words; in her answers are mildness and truth.

Submission and obedience are the lessons of her life; and peace and happiness are her reward.

Before her steps walketh Prudence; and Virtue attendeth at her right-hand.

Her eye speaketh softness and love; but discretion with a sceptre sitteth on her brow.

The tongue of the licentious is dumb in her presence; the awe of her virtue keepeth him silent.

When scandal is busy, and the fame of her neighbour is tossed from tongue to tongue, if charity and good-nature open not her mouth, the finger of silence resteth on her lip.

Her breast is the mansion of goodness; and therefore she suspecteth no evil in others.

Happy were the man that should make her his wife; happy the child that shall call her mother.

She presideth in the house, and there is peace; she commandeth with judgment, and is obeyed.

She ariseth in the morning; she considers her affairs; and appointeth to every one their proper business.

The care of her family is her whole delight; to that alone she applieth her study; and elegance with frugality is seen in her mansions.

The

The prudence of her management is an honour to her husband, and he heareth her praise with silent delight.

She informeth the minds of her children with wisdom; she fashioneth their manners from the example of her own goodness.

The word of her mouth is the law of her youth; the motion of her eye commandeth their obedience.

She speaketh, and her servants fly; she pointeth, and the thing is done: for the law of love is in their hearts; her kindness addeth wings to their feet.

In prosperity she is not puffed up; in adversity she healeth the wounds of fortune with patience.

The troubles of her husband are alleviated by her counsels, and sweetened by her endearments; he putteth his heart in her bosom, and receiveth comfort.

Happy is the man that hath made her his wife; happy the child that calleth her mother.

BOOK

BOOK IV.
CONSANGUINITY, or Natural RELATIONS.

CHAP. I.
HUSBAND.

TAKE unto thyself a wife, and obey the ordinance of God; take unto thyself a wife, and become a faithful member of society.

But examine with care, and fix not suddenly: on thy present choice depends the future happiness of thee and thy posterity.

If much of her time is destroyed in dress and adornments, if she is enamour'd with her own beauty, and delighted with her own praise, if she laugheth much, and talketh aloud, if her foot abideth not in her father's house, and her eyes with boldness rove on the faces of men? though her beauty were as the sun in the firmament of heaven, turn thine eyes from her charms, turn thy feet from her paths, and suffer not thy soul to be ensnared by the allurements of thy imagination.

But when thou findest sensibility of heart join'd with softness of manners, an accomplished mind, with a form agreeable to thy fancy, take her home to thy house; she is worthy to be thy friend, thy companion in life, the wife of thy bosom.

O cherish her as a blessing sent thee from heaven; let the kindness of thy behaviour endear thee to her heart.

She is the mistress of thy house; treat her therefore with respect, that thy servants may obey her.

Oppose not her inclination without cause; she is the partner of thy cares, make her also the companion of thy pleasures.

Reprove her faults with gentleness: exact not her obedience with rigour.

Trust thy secrets in her breast; her counsels are sincere; thou shalt not be deceived.

Be faithful to her bed; for she is the mother of thy children.

When pain and sickness assault her, let thy tenderness sooth her affliction: a look from thee of pity and love, shall alleviate her grief, or mitigate her pain; and be of more avail than ten physicians.

Consider the delicacy of her sex, the tenderness of her frame; and be not severe to her weakness, but remember thine own imperfections.

CHAP. II.

FATHER.

COnsider, thou who art a parent, the importance of thy trust; the being thou hast produced, it is thy duty to support.

Upon thee also it dependeth, whether

ther the child of thy bosom shall be a blessing or a curse to thyself; a useful or a worthless member of the community.

Prepare him with early instruction, and season his mind with the maxims of truth.

Watch the bent of his inclination; set him right in his youth; and let no evil habit gain strength with his years.

So shall he rise like a cedar on the mountains; his head shall be seen above the trees of the forest.

A wicked son is a reproach to his father; but he that doeth right is an honour to his grey hairs.

The soil is thine own, let it not want cultivation; the seed which thou sowest, that also shalt thou reap.

Teach him obedience, and he shall bless thee; teach him modesty, and he shall not be ashamed.

Teach him gratitude, and he shall receive benefits; teach him charity, and he shall gain love.

Teach him temperance, and he shall have health; teach him prudence, and fortune shall attend him.

Teach him justice, and he shall be honoured by the world; teach him sincerity, and his own heart shall not reproach him.

Teach him diligence, and his wealth shall increase; teach him benevolence, and his mind shall be exalted.

Teach him science, and his life shall be useful; teach him religion, and his death shall be happy.

CHAP. III.
SON.

FROM the creatures of God let man learn wisdom, and apply to himself the instruction they give.

Go to the desart, my son; observe the young stork of the wilderness; let him speak to thy heart. He beareth on his wings his aged sire; he lodgeth him in safety, and supplieth him with food. The

The piety of a child is sweeter than the incense of *Persia* offered to the sun; yea more delicious than odours wasted from a field of *Arabian* spices by the western gales.

Be grateful then to thy father, for he gave thee life; and to thy mother, for she sustained thee.

Hear the words of his mouth, for they are spoken for thy good; give ear to his admonition, for it proceedeth from love.

He hath watched for thy welfare, he hath toiled for thy ease; do honour therefore to his age, and let not his grey hairs be treated with irreverence.

Think on thy helpless infancy, and the frowardness of thy youth, and indulge the infirmities of thy aged parents; assist and support them in the decline of life.

So shall their hoary heads go down to the grave in peace; and thine own children, in reverence of thy example, shall repay thy piety with filial love.

CHAP. IV.

BROTHERS.

YE are the children of one father, provided for by his care; and the breast of one mother hath given you suck.

Let the bonds of affection, therefore, unite thee with thy brothers; that peace and happiness may dwell in thy father's house.

And, when ye separate in the world, remember the relation that bindeth you to love and unity: prefer not a stranger before thine own blood.

If thy brother is in adversity, assist him; if thy sister is in trouble, forsake her not.

So shall the fortunes of thy father contribute to the support of his whole race, and his care be continued to you all in your love to each other.

BOOK V.
PROVIDENCE; or, The accidental Differences of MEN.

CHAP. I.
WISE and IGNORANT.

THE gifts of the understanding are the treasures of God; and he appointeth to every one his portion, in what measure seemeth good unto himself.

Hath he endow'd thee with wisdom? hath he enlighten'd thy mind with the knowledge of truth? communicate it to the ignorant for their instruction; communicate it to the wise for their own improvement.

True wisdom is less presuming than folly; the wise man doubteth often, and changeth his mind; the fool is obstinate, and doubteth not; he knoweth all things, but his own ignorance.

The pride of emptiness is an abomination, and to talk much is the foolishness of folly; nevertheless it is the part of wisdom to bear the impertinence of fools, to hear their absurdities with patience, and pity their weakness.

Yet be not puffed up in thine own conceit, neither boast of superior understanding; the clearest human knowledge is but blindness and folly.

The wise man seeeth his imperfections, and is humbled; he laboureth in vain for his own approbation. But the fool peepeth in the shallow stream of his own mind, and is pleased with the pebbles which he seeth at the bottom: he bringeth them up and sheweth them as pearls; and with the applause of his brethren delighteth he himself.

He boasteth of attainments in things of no worth: but where it is a shame to be ignorant, there he hath no understanding.

Even in the paths of wisdom he toileth

eth after folly; and shame and disappointment are the reward of his labour.

But the wise man cultivateth his mind with knowledge; the improvement of arts is his delight; and their utility to the public crowneth him with honour.

Nevertheless, the attainment of virtue he accounteth as the highest learning: and the science of happiness is the study of his life.

CHAP. II.

RICH and POOR.

THE man to whom God hath given riches, and a mind to employ them aright, is peculiarly favoured and highly distinguished.

He looketh on his wealth with pleasure; because it affordeth him the means to do good.

He protecteth the poor, that are injured; he suffereth not the mighty to oppress the weak.

He seeketh out objects of compassion; he enquireth into their wants; he relieveth them with judgment, and without ostentation.

He assisteth and rewardeth merit; he encourageth ingenuity, and liberally promoteth every useful design.

He carrieth on great works; his country is enriched; and the labourer is employ'd; he formeth new schemes, and the arts receive improvement.

He considereth the superfluities of his table as belonging to the poor, and he defraudeth them not.

The benevolence of his mind is not check'd by his fortune. He rejoiceth therefore in riches, and his joy is blameless.

But woe unto him that heapeth up wealth in abundance, and rejoiceth alone in the possession thereof.

That grindeth the face of the poor, and considereth not the sweat of their brows.

He thriveth on oppression without feeling; the ruin of his brother disturbeth him not.

The tears of the orphan he drinketh as milk; the cries of the widow are music to his ear.

His heart is harden'd with the love of wealth; no grief or distress can make impression upon it.

But the curse of iniquity pursueth him; he liveth in continual fear. The anxiety of his mind, and the rapacious desires of his own soul, take vengeance upon him, for the calamities he hath brought upon others.

O! what are the miseries of poverty, in comparison with the gnawings of this man's heart.

Let the poor man comfort himself, yea, rejoice; for he hath many reasons.

He sitteth down to his morsel in peace; his table is not crowded with flatterers and devourers.

He is not embarrassed with dependents,

dents, nor teased with the clamours of solicitation.

Debarr'd from the dainties of the rich, he escapeth also their diseases.

The bread that he eateth, is it not sweet to his taste? the water he drinketh, is it not pleasant to his thirst? yea far more delicious than the richest draughts of the luxurious.

His labour preserveth his health, and produceth him a repose, to which the downy bed of sloth is a stranger.

He limiteth his desires with humility; and the calm of contentment is sweeter to his soul than the acquirements of wealth and grandeur.

Let not the rich therefore presume on his riches, nor the poor despond in his poverty: for the providence of God dispenseth happiness to them both; and the distribution thereof is more equally made, than the fool can believe.

CHAP.

CHAP. III.

MASTERS and SERVANTS.

REPINE not, O man, that thou servest another: it is the appointment of God, and hath many advantages; it removeth thee from the cares and solicitudes of life.

The honour of a servant is his fidelity: his highest virtues are submission and obedience.

Be patient therefore under the reproofs of thy master; and when he rebuketh thee, answer not again: the silence of thy resignation shall not be forgotten.

Be studious of his interests; be diligent in his affairs; and faithful to the trust which he reposeth in thee.

Thy time and thy labour belong unto him; defraud him not thereof, for he payeth thee for them.

And thou, who art a master, be just to thy servant, if thou expectest fidelity; be reasonable in thy commands, if thou expectest obedience.

The spirit of a man is in him; severity and rigour, which create fear, cannot command his love.

Mix kindness with reproof, and reason with authority; so shall thy admonitions take place in his heart, and his duty shall become his pleasure.

He shall serve thee faithfully from gratitude; he shall obey thee chearfully from love; and fail not thou in return to give his diligence and fidelity their just reward.

CHAP. IV.

Magistrates *and* Subjects.

O Thou, the favourite of heaven, whom the sons of men, thy equals, have raised to sovereign power, and set as a ruler over themselves; consider the

the ends and importance of their trust, far more than the dignity and height of thy station.

Thou art cloathed in purple; thou art seated on a throne; the crown of majesty investeth thy temples; the sceptre of power is placed in thy hand: but not for thyself were these ensigns given; nor meant for thy own, but the good of thy kingdom.

The glory of a king is the welfare of his people; his power and dominion resteth on the hearts of his subjects.

The mind of a great prince is exalted with the grandeur of his situation; he revolveth high things, and searcheth for business worthy of his power.

He calleth together the wise men of his kingdom; he consulteth amongst them with freedom, and heareth the opinion of them all.

He looketh among his people with discernment; he discovereth the abilities of men, and employeth them according to their merits.

His

His magistrates are just; his ministers are wise; and the favourite of his bosom deceiveth him not.

He smileth on the arts, and they flourish; the sciences improve beneath the culture of his hand.

With the learned and ingenious he delighteth himself; he kindleth in their breasts emulation: and the glory of his kingdom is exalted by their labours.

The spirit of the merchant who extendeth his commerce, the skill of the farmer who enricheth his lands, the ingenuity of the artist, the improvements of the scholar, all these he honoureth with his favour, or rewardeth with his bounty.

He planteth new colonies; he buildeth strong ships; he openeth rivers for convenience; he formeth harbours for safety; his people abound in riches; and the strength of his kingdom increaseth.

He frameth his statutes with equity and wisdom; his subjects enjoy the

fruits

fruits of their labour in security, and their happiness consists in their observance of the law.

He foundeth his judgments on the principles of mercy; but in the punishment of offenders he is strict and impartial.

His ears are open to the complaints of his subjects; he restraineth the hand of oppressors; and delivereth them from their tyranny.

His people therefore look up to him as a father, with reverence and love; they consider him as the guardian of all they enjoy.

Their affection unto him begetteth in his breast a love of the public; the security of their happiness is the object of his care.

No murmurs against him arise in their hearts; the machinations of his enemies endanger not his state.

His subjects are faithful and firm in his cause; they stand in his defence as a wall of brass. The army of his enemy flieth before them as chaff before the wind.

Security and peace bless the dwellings of his people; and glory and strength encircle his throne for ever.

BOOK

BOOK VI.
The SOCIAL DUTIES.

CHAP. I.
BENEVOLENCE.

WHEN thou considerest thy wants, when thou beholdest thy imperfections, acknowledge his goodness, O man! who honour'd thee with reason, endow'd thee with speech, and placed thee in society to receive and confer reciprocal helps and mutual obligations.

Thy food, thy cloathing, thy convenience of habitation, thy protection from the injuries, thy enjoyment of the comforts and the pleasures of life, thou owest to the assistance of others; and couldst not enjoy but in the bands of society.

It is thy duty therefore to be friendly to mankind, as it is thy interest that men should be friendly to thee.

As the rose breatheth sweetness from its own nature, so the heart of a benevolent man produceth good works.

He enjoyeth the ease and tranquility of his own breast; and rejoiceth in the happiness and prosperity of his neighbour.

He openeth not his ear unto slander; the faults and the failings of men give pain to his heart.

His desire is to do good, and he searcheth out the occasions thereof: in removing the oppression of another he relieveth himself.

From the largeness of his mind, he comprehendeth in his wishes the happiness of all men; and from the generosity of his heart he endeavoureth to promote it.

CHAP.

CHAP. II.
JUSTICE.

THE peace of society dependeth on justice; the happiness of individuals on the certain enjoyment of all their possessions.

Keep the desires of thy heart, therefore, within the bounds of moderation; let the hand of justice lead them aright.

Cast not an evil eye on the goods of thy neighbour; let whatever is his property, be sacred from thy touch.

Let not temptation allure, nor any provocation excite thee to lift up thy hand to the hazard of his life.

Defame him not in his character; bear no false witness against him.

Corrupt not his servant to cheat or forsake him; and the wife of his bosom, O tempt not to sin.

'Twill be a grief to his heart, which thou canst not relieve; an injury to his life, which no reparation can atone.

In thy dealings with men be impartial and just; and do unto them, as thou wouldst they should do unto thee.

Be faithful to thy trust; and deceive not the man who relieth upon thee; be assured 'tis less in the sight of God to steal, than to betray.

Oppress not the poor, and defraud not of his hire the labouring man.

When thou sellest for gain, hear the whisperings of Conscience; and be satisfy'd with moderation; nor from the ignorance of the buyer make advantage to thyself.

Pay the debts which thou owest; for he who gave thee credit relied upon thy honour; and to with-hold from him his due, is both mean and unjust.

Finally, O son of society, examine thy heart; call remembrance to thy aid: and, if in any of these things thou findest thou hast transgressed, take sorrow and shame to thyself; and make speedy reparation to the utmost of thy power.

CHAP. III.
CHARITY.

HAPPY is the man who hath sown in his breast the seeds of benevolence; the produce thereof shall be charity and love.

From the fountain of his heart shall rise rivers of goodness; and the streams shall overflow for the benefit of mankind.

He assisteth the poor in their trouble; he rejoiceth in furthering the prosperity of all men.

He censureth not his neighbour; he believeth not the tales of envy and malevolence; neither repeateth he their slanders.

He forgiveth the injuries of men; he wipeth them from his remembrance; revenge and malice have no place in his heart.

For evil he returneth not evil; he hateth not even his enemies; but requiteth quieteth their injustice with friendly admonition.

The griefs and anxieties of men excite his compassion; he endeavoureth to alleviate the weight of their misfortunes; and the pleasure of success rewardeth his labour.

He calmeth the fury, he healeth the quarrels of angry men; and preventeth the mischiefs of strife and animosity.

He promoteth in his neighbourhood peace and good-will; and his name is repeated with praise and benedictions.

CHAP. IV.
GRATITUDE.

AS the branches of a tree return their sap to the root, from whence it arose; as a river poureth his streams to the sea, whence his spring was supply'd; so the heart of a grateful man delighteth in returning a benefit received.

He acknowledgeth his obligation with

with chearfulness; he looketh on his benefactor with love and esteem.

And, if to return it be not in his power, he nourisheth the memory of it in his breast with kindness; he forgetteth it not all the days of his life.

The hand of the generous man is like the clouds of heaven, which drop upon the earth fruits, herbage, and flowers: the heart of the ungrateful is like a desart of sand, which swalloweth with greediness the showers that fall, but burieth them in his bosom, and produceth nothing.

Envy not thy benefactor; neither strive to conceal the benefit he hath conferred; for, though to oblige is better than to be obliged, though the act of generosity commandeth admiration; yet the humility of gratitude toucheth the heart, and is amiable in the sight both of God and man.

But receive not a favour from the hand of the proud; to the selfish and avaricious have no obligation: the vanity of Pride shall expose thee to shame; the greediness of Avarice shall never be satisfy'd.

CHAP. V.

SINCERITY.

O Thou that art enamour'd with the beauties of Truth, and hast fixed thy heart on the simplicity of her charms, hold fast thy fidelity unto her, and forsake her not: the constancy of thy virtue shall crown thee with honour.

The tongue of the sincere is rooted in his heart; hypocrisy and deceit have no place in his words.

He blusheth at falshood, and is confounded: but in speaking the truth he hath a steady eye.

He supporteth as a man the dignity of his character; to the arts of hypocrisy he scorneth to stoop.

He is consistent with himself; he is never embarrassed; he hath courage in truth, but to lie he is afraid.

He

He is far above the meanness of dissimulation; the words of his mouth are the thoughts of his heart.

Yet with prudence and caution he openeth his lips: he studieth what is right, and speaketh with discretion.

He adviseth in friendship; he reproveth with freedom; and whatsoever he promiseth shall surely be performed.

But the heart of the hypocrite is hid in his breast. He masketh his words in the semblance of truth, while the business of his life is only to deceive.

He laugheth in sorrow; he weepeth in joy; and the words of his mouth have no interpretation.

He worketh in the dark as a mole, and fancieth he is safe: but he blundereth into light, and is expos'd to full view, with his dirt on his head.

He passeth his days in perpetual constraint; his tongue and his heart are for ever at variance.

He laboureth for the character of a righteous man; and huggeth himself in the thoughts of his cunning.

O fool, fool! the pains which thou takest to hide what thou art, are more than would make thee what thou wouldst seem; the children of wisdom shall mock at thy cunning; and when thy disguise is stripped off, the finger of derision shall point thee to scorn.

BOOK

BOOK VII.

RELIGION.

THERE is but one God, the author, the creator, the governor of the world, almighty, eternal, and incomprehensible.

The sun is not God, tho' his noblest image. He enlighteneth the world with his brightness; his warmth giveth life to the products of the earth: admire him as the creature, the instrument of God; but worship him not.

To the One who is supreme, most wise, and beneficent, and to him alone, belong worship, adoration, thanksgiving, and praise.

Who hath stretched forth the heavens with his hand; who hath described with his finger the courses of the stars.

Who setteth bounds to the ocean, which it cannot pass; and saith unto the stormy winds, Be still.

Who

Who shaketh the earth, and the nations tremble; who darteth his lightnings, and the wicked are dismayed.

Who calleth forth worlds by the word of his mouth; who smiteth with his arm, and they sink into nothing.

"O reverence the majesty of the "Omnipotent! and tempt not his an- "ger, lest thou be destroyed."

The providence of God is over all his works; he ruleth and directeth with infinite wisdom.

He hath instituted laws for the government of the world; he hath wonderfully varied them in all beings; and each, by his nature, conformeth to his will.

In the depth of his mind he revolveth all knowledge; the secrets of futurity lie open before him.

The thoughts of thy heart are naked to his view; he knoweth thy determinations before they are made.

With respect to his prescience, there is nothing contingent; with respect to

his

his providence, there is nothing accidental.

Wonderful he is in all his ways; his counsels are inscrutable; the manner of his knowledge transcendeth thy conception.

"Pay, therefore, to his wisdom all "honour and veneration; and bow "down thyself in humble and submis- "sive obedience to his supreme direc- "tion."

The Lord is gracious and beneficent: he hath created the world in mercy and love.

His goodness is conspicuous in all his works; he is the fountain of excellence, the centre of perfection.

The creatures of his hand declare his goodness, and all their enjoyments speak his praise: he cloatheth them with beauty, he supporteth them with food; he preserveth them with pleasure from generation to generation.

If we lift up our eyes to the heavens, his glory shineth forth; if we cast them

them down upon the earth, it is full of his goodness; the hills and the vallies rejoice and sing; fields, rivers, and woods resound his praise.

But thee, O man, he hath distinguished with peculiar favour, and exalted thy station above all creatures.

He hath endowed thee with reason to maintain thy dominion; he hath fitted thee with language, to improve by society; and exalted thy mind with the powers of meditation, to contemplate and adore his inimitable perfections.

And in the laws he hath ordained as the rule of thy life, so kindly hath he suited thy duty to thy nature, that obedience to his precepts is happiness to thyself.

" O praise his goodness with songs
" of thanksgiving, and meditate in si-
" lence on the wonders of his love:
" let thy heart overflow with grati-
" tude and acknowledgment; let the
" lan-

"language of thy lips speak praise and
"adoration; let the actions of thy life
"show thy love to his law."

The Lord is just and righteous; and will judge the earth with equity and truth.

Hath he established his laws in goodness and mercy, and shall he not punish the transgressors thereof?

O think not, bold man! because thy punishment is delay'd, that the arm of the Lord is weaken'd; neither flatter thyself with hopes that he winketh at thy doings.

His eye pierceth the secrets of every heart, and he remembereth them for ever: he respecteth not the persons, nor the stations of men.

The high and the low, the rich and the poor, the wise and the ignorant; when the soul hath shaken off the cumbrous shackles of this mortal life, shall equally receive from the sentence of of God a just and everlasting retribution according to their works.

Then shall the wicked tremble and be afraid; but the heart of the righteous shall rejoice in his judgments.

"O fear the Lord, therefore, all the "days of thy life; and walk in the "paths which he hath opened before "thee. Let Prudence admonish thee; "let Temperance restrain; let Justice "guide thy hand, Benevolence warm "thy heart, and Gratitude to heaven "inspire thee with devotion. These "shall give thee happiness in thy pre- "sent state, and bring thee to the "mansions of eternal felicity in the "paradise of God."

This is the true ŒCONOMY of HUMAN LIFE.

THE
OECONOMY
OF
HUMAN LIFE.

TRANSLATED

From an INDIAN MANUSCRIPT, found soon after that which contained the Original of the First Part; and written by the same Hand.

IN

A Second LETTER from an English Gentleman, residing in China, to the Earl of Chesterfield.

PART THE SECOND.

COVENTRY:
Printed and Sold by M. LUCKMAN.
M DCC LXXXVII.

TO THE

Earl of *Chesterfield*.

Peking, Jan. 10, 1749-50.

MY LORD,

NOT a month after I had inclosed to your Lordship the translation I had attempted of the *Oriental System of Morality*, so famous in these parts, we were agreeably surprized with a manuscript of the same size, whose Antiquity, Characters, and other internal marks, determined it to be the performance of that author, which, at the same time that it shewed us something was wanting to what we had before esteemed a complete system, very happily supplied the deficiency.

G I could

I could not rest, after the first dipping into it, without undertaking the pleasing task of a Translation; nor, when I had finished it, without doing myself the honour of transmitting it to your Lordship. I need not tell your Lordship, that the energy of thought, sublimity of style, and many other circumstances, prove it to come from the divine hand that planned the other: the substance of it carries abundantly more proof of it.

If I did not flatter myself that the *First Part* had met the honour of your Lordship's approbation, I should not be so earnest in dispatching this after it: but while I know the value of the work, and know your Lordship's distinguishing genius, it would be ridiculous to affect a doubt about it.

I am, my LORD,

Your's, &c.

BOOK I.
MAN considered in the general.

CHAP. I.
Of the HUMAN FRAME and STRUCTURE.

WEAK and ignorant as thou art, O man! humble as thou oughtest to be, O child of the dust! wouldst thou raise thy thoughts to infinite Wisdom? wouldst thou see Omnipotence displayed before thee? contemplate thine own frame.

Fearfully and wonderfully art thou made: praise therefore thy Creator with awe, and rejoice before him with reverence.

Wherefore of all creatures art thou only erect; but that thou shouldst behold his works! Wherefore art thou to behold; but that thou mayst admire them! Wherefore to admire; but that thou mayst adore their, and thy Creator!

Wherefore is consciousness reposed in thee alone; and whence is it derived to thee?

'Tis not in flesh to think; 'tis not in bones to reason: the lion knoweth not that worms shall eat him: the ox perceiveth not that he is fed for slaughter.

Something is added to thee unlike to what thou feest: something informs thy clay, higher than all that is the object of thy senses. Behold! what is it?

Thy body remaineth perfect after this is fled; therefore it is no part of the body: it is immaterial; therefore eternal: it is free to act; therefore accountable for its actions.

Knoweth the ass the use of food, because his teeth mow down the herbage?

bage? or standeth the crocodile erect, although his back-bone is strait as thine?

God formed thee as he had formed these: after them all wast thou created: superiority and command were given thee over all: and of his own breath did he communicate to thee thy principle of knowledge.

Know thyself then the pride of his creation; the link uniting divinity and matter: behold a part of God himself within thee: remember thine own dignity; nor dare to descend unto evil.

Who planted terror in the tail of the serpent? who cloathed the neck of the horse with thunder? even he who hath instructed thee to crush the one under thy feet, and to tame the other to thy purposes.

CHAP. II.

Of the USE *of the* SENSES.

VAUNT not of thy body, because it was first formed; nor of thy brain, because therein thy soul resideth. Is not the master of the house more honourable than its walls?

The ground must be prepared before corn be planted: the potter must build his furnace before he can make his porcelane.

As the breath of heaven sayeth unto the water of the deep, this way shall thy billows roll, and no other; thus high shall they raise their fury, and no higher: so let thy spirit, O man, actuate and direct thy flesh; so let thy spirit bring it into subjection.

Thy soul is the monarch of thy frame: suffer not its subjects to rebel against it.

Thy body is as the globe of the earth: thy bones the pillars that sustain it on its basis.

As the ocean giveth rise to springs, whose waters return again into its bosom thro' the rivers: so runneth thy life from the heart outwards, and so returneth it unto its place again.

Do not both retain their course for ever? Behold, the same God ordained them.

Is not thy nose the channel to perfumes? thy mouth the path to delicacies? yet know thou, that perfumes long smelt become offensive; and delicacies destroy the appetite they flatter.

Are not thine eyes the centinels that watch for thee? yet how often are they unable to distinguish truth from error? keep then thy soul in moderation, teach thy spirit to be attentive to its good: so shall these its ministers be ever unto thee conveyances of truth.

Thine hand is it not a miracle? is there in the creation aught like unto it?

wherefore was it given thee; but that thou mightest stretch it out to the assistance of thy brother?

Why of all things living art thou alone made capable of blushing? The world shall read thy shame upon thy face, therefore do nothing shameful.

Fear and dismay, why rob they thy countenance of its ruddy splendour? Avoid guilt and thou shalt know that fear is beneath thee, that dismay is unmanly.

Wherefore to thee alone speak shadows in the visions of thy pillow? Reverence them; for know that dreams are from on high.

Thou man alone can speak; wonder at thy glorious prerogative, and pay to him who gave thee speech a rational and welcome praise: teach also thy children wisdom; instruct the offspring of thy loins in piety.

CHAP.

CHAP. III.

The SOUL of MAN, its Origin and Affections.

THE blessings, O man! of thy external part are health, vigour and proportion; the greatest of these is health. What health is to the body even that is honesty to the soul.

That thou hast a soul is of all knowledge the most certain; of all truths the most plain unto thee: be meek; be grateful for it; seek not to know it perfectly; it is inscrutable.

Thought, understanding, reason, will;—call not these thy soul! they are its actions, but they are not its essence.

Raise it not too high that thou be not despised: be not thou like unto those who fall by climbing; neither debase it to the sense of brutes: nor be thou like to the horse and the mule, in whom there is no understanding.

Search it by its faculties; know it by its virtues: they are more in number than the hairs of thy head; the stars of heaven are not to be counted with them.

Think not with *Arabia* that one soul is parted among all men; neither believe thou with the sons of *Egypt*, that every man hath many: know that as thy heart so is thy soul also one.

Doth not the sun harden the clay? doth it not also soften the wax? As it is one sun that worketh both, even so it is one soul that willeth contraries.

As the moon retaineth her nature tho' darkness spread itself before her face as a curtain; so the soul remaineth perfect even in the bosom of the fool.

She is immortal: she is unchangeable; she is alike in all: health calleth her forth to shew her loveliness; and application anointeth her with the oil of wisdom.

Altho' she shall live after thee, think not she was born before thee: she was
created

created with thy flesh, and formed with thy brain.

Justice could not give her to thee exalted by virtues, nor mercy deliver her to thee deformed by vices. These must be thine, and thou must answer them.

Suppose not death can shield thee from examination; think not corruption can hide thee from enquiry. He who formed thee of thou knowest not what, can he not raise thee from thou knowest not what again?

Perceiveth not the cock the hour of midnight? exalteth he not his voice, to tell thee when it is morning? Knoweth not the dog the footsteps of his master? and flieth not the wounded goat unto the herb that healeth him? yet when these die, their spirit returneth to the dust: thine alone surviveth.

Envy not to these their senses, because quicker than thine own: learn that the advantage lieth not in possessing good things, but in the knowing how to use them.

Hadst

Hadst thou the ear of the stag; or were thine eye as strong and piercing as the eagle's; didst thou equal the hound in smell; or could the ape resign to thee his taste; or the tortoise her feeling; yet without reason what would they avail thee? Perish not all these like their kindred?

Hath any one of them the gift of speech? Can any say unto thee, Therefore did I so?

The lips of the wise are as the doors of a cabinet; no sooner are they opened, but treasures are poured out before thee.

Like unto trees of gold arranged in beds of silver, are wise sentences uttered in due season.

Canst thou think too greatly of thy soul? or can too much be said in its praise? It is the image of him who gave it.

Remember thou its dignity for ever; forget not how great a talent is committed to thy charge.

Whatsoever may do good, may also do harm: beware that thou direct its course to virtue.

Think not that thou canst lose her in the croud: suppose not that thou canst bury her in thy closet: action is her delight, and she will not be withheld from it.

Her motion is perpetual; her attempts are universal: her agility is not to be suppress'd; is it at the uttermost part of the earth? she will have it: is it beyond the region of the stars? yet will her eye discover it.

Inquiry is her delight: as one who traverseth the burning sands in search of water, so is the soul that thirsteth after knowledge.

Guard her for she is rash; restrain her for she is irregular: correct her for she is outrageous: more unstable is she than water; more flexible than wax; more yielding than air: is there aught then can bind her?

As a sword in the hand of a madman; even so is the soul to him who wanteth discretion.

The end of her search is truth; her means to discover it are reason and experience: but are not these weak, uncertain and fallacious? how then shall she attain unto it?

General opinion is no proof of truth, for the generality of men are ignorant.

Perception of thyself; the knowledge of him who created thee; the sense of the worship thou owest unto him; are not these plain before thy face? and behold! what is there more that man needeth to know?

CHAP. IV.

Of the PERIOD *and* USES *of* HUMAN LIFE.

AS the eye of the morning to the lark; as the shade of the evening to the owl; as honey to the bee, or as the carcase to the vulture; even such is life unto the heart of man.

Tho' bright it dazzleth not; tho' obscure it displeaseth not; tho' sweet it cloyeth not; tho' corrupt it forbiddeth not: yet who is he that knoweth its true value?

Learn to esteem life as thou oughtest; then art thou near the pinnacle of wisdom.

Think not with the fool that nothing is more valuable; nor believe with the pretended wise, that thou oughtest to contemn it: love not life for itself, but for the good it may be of to others.

Gold cannot buy it for thee: neither can mines of diamonds purchase back the

112   The Oeconomy   Part II.
the moment thou hast now lost of it;
employ thy succeeding ones in virtue.

Say not that it were best not to have
been born; or if born, that it had been
best to die early: neither dare thou to
ask of thy Creator, Where had been
the evil had I not existed? Good is in
thy power: the want of good, is evil:
and if thy question be just, lo! it condemneth thee.

Would the fish swallow the bait if
he knew the hook was hid therein?
Would the lion enter the toils if he saw
they were prepared for him? so neither were the soul to perish with this
clay, would man wish to live; neither
would a merciful God have created
him: know hence thou shalt live af-
terward.

As the bird enclosed in the cage before he seeth it, yet teareth not his
flesh against its sides; so neither labour
thou vainly to run from the state thou
art in, but know it is allotted thee;
and be content with it.

Tho'

Tho' its ways are uneven, yet are they not all painful; accommodate thyself to all; and where there is least appearance of evil, suspect the greatest danger.

When thy bed is straw, thou sleepest in security; but when thou stretchest thyself on roses, beware of the thorns.

A good death is better than an evil life; strive to live therefore as long as thou oughtest, not as long as thou canst: while thy life is to others worth more than thy death, it is thy duty to preserve it.

Complain not with the fool of the shortness of thy time; remember that with thy days thy cares are shortened.

Take from the period of thy life the useless parts of it; and what remaineth? Take off the time of thine infancy, the second infancy of age, thy sleep, thy thoughtless hours, thy days of sickness; and even at the fulness of years, how few seasons hast thou truly numbered.

He who gave thee life as a blessing, shortened it to make it more so: to what end would longer life have served thee? wishest thou to have had an opportunity of more vices? as to the good, will not he who limited thy span, be satisfied with the fruits of it?

To what end, O child of sorrow, would'st thou live longer? to breathe, to eat, to see the world? all this thou hast done often already; too frequent repetition, is it not tiresome? or is it not superfluous?

Would'st thou improve thy wisdom and thy virtue? alas! what art thou to know? or who is it that shall teach thee? badly thou employest the little thou hast; dare not therefore to complain that more is not given thee.

Repine not at the want of knowledge, it must perish with thee in the grave; be honest here, thou shalt be wise hereafter.

Say not unto the crow, why numberest thou seven times the age of thy lord?

or to the fawn, why are thine eyes to see my offspring to an hundred generations? are these to be compared with thee in the abuse of life? are they riotous? are they cruel? are they ungrateful? learn from them rather that innocence of life and simplicity of manners are the paths to a good old age.

Knowest thou to employ life better than these? then less of it may suffice thee.

Man, who dares enslave the world, when he knows that he can enjoy his tyranny but for a moment; what would he not aim at were he immortal?

Enough hast thou of life, but thou regardest not: thou art not in want of it, O man! but thou art prodigal; thou throwest it lightly away, as if thou hadst more than enough; and yet thou repinest that it is not gathered again unto thee.

Know that it is not abundance which maketh rich, but œconomy.

The wise continueth to live from his first period: the fool is always beginning.

Labour not after riches first, and think thou afterwards wilt enjoy them: he who neglecteth the present moment, throweth away all that he hath: as the arrow passeth through the heart, while the warrior knew not that it was coming; so shall his life be taken away before he knoweth that he hath it.

What then is life, that man should desire it? and what is breathing, that he should covet it?

Is it not a scene of delusion? a series of misadventures; a pursuit of evils linked on all sides together; in the beginning it is ignorance, pain is in its middle, and its end is sorrow.

As one wave pusheth on another, till both are involved in that behind them; even so succeedeth evil to evil in the life of man; the greater and the present swallow up the lesser and the past: Our terrors are real evils: our expectations look forward into improbabilities.

Fools

Fools, to dread as mortals; and to desire as if immortal!

What part of life is it that we would wish to remain with us? Is it youth? can we be in love with outrage, licentiousness and temerity? Is it age? then are we fond of infirmities.

It is said grey hairs are revered, and in length of days is honour. Virtue can add reverence to the bloom of youth; and without it age plants more wrinkles in the soul than on the forehead.

Is age respected because it hateth riot? What justice is in this? when it is not age despiseth pleasure, but pleasure that despiseth age.

Be virtuous while thou art young, so shall thine age be honoured.

BOOK II.

MAN considered in regard to his Infirmities, and their Effects.

CHAP. I.
VANITY.

INconstancy is powerful in the heart of man; intemperance swayeth it whither it will; despair ingrosseth much of it; and fear proclaimeth, Behold I sit unrivalled therein. But vanity is beyond them all.

Weep not therefore at the calamities of the human state; rather smile at its follies. In the hands of the man addicted to vanity, life is but the shadow of a dream.

The hero, the most renowned of human characters, what is he but a bubble of this weakness? the public is unstable and ungrateful! Why should the man of wisdom endanger himself for fools?

The man who neglecteth his present concerns, to revolve how he will behave when he is greater, feedeth himself with wind, while his bread is eaten by another.

Act as becometh thee in thy present station: and in a more exalted one thy face shall not be ashamed.

What blindeth the eye, or what hideth the heart of a man from himself, like vanity? lo! when thou seest not thyself, then others discover thee most plainly.

As the tulip that is gaudy without smell, conspicuous without use; so is the man who setteth himself up on high, and hath no merit.

The heart of the Vain is troubled while it seemeth content: his cares are greater than his pleasures.

His solicitude cannot rest with his bones: the grave is not deep enough to hide it: he extendeth his thoughts beyond his being: he bespeaketh praise, to be paid when he is gone: but whoso promiseth it, deceiveth him.

As the man who engageth his wife to remain in widowhood that she disturb not his soul; so is he who expecteth that praise shall reach his ears beneath the earth, or cherish his heart in its shroud.

Do well whilst thou livest; but regard not what is said of it: content thyself with deserving praise, and thy posterity shall rejoice in hearing it.

As the butterfly, who seeth not her own colours; as the jessamine, which scenteth not the odour it casteth around; so is the man who appeareth gay, and biddeth others to take note of it.

To what purpose, saith he, is my vesture of gold, to what end are my tables filled with dainties, if no eye gaze upon them, if the world know it not? Give thy raiment to the naked: and thy food unto the hungry; so shalt thou be praised;

Part II. of HUMAN LIFE.

praised; and shalt feel that thou deservest it.

Why bestowest thou on every man the flattery of unmeaning words? thou knowest that when returned unto thee thou regardest it not. He knoweth he lieth unto thee: yet he knoweth thou wilt thank him for it. Speak in sincerity, and thou shalt hear with instruction.

The vain delighteth to speak of himself; but he seeth not that others like not to hear him.

If he hath done any thing worthy of praise; if he possess that which is worthy of admiration; his joy is to proclaim it; his pride is to hear it reported. The desire of such a man defeateth itself: men say not, behold he hath done it; or see he possesseth it; but mark how proud he is of it.

The heart of man cannot attend at once to many things: he who fixeth his soul on shew, loseth reality: he pursueth

sueth bubbles which break in their flight, while he treads to earth what would do him honour.

CHAP. II.
INCONSTANCY.

NATURE urgeth thee to Inconstancy, O man! therefore guard thyself at all times against it.

Thou art from the womb of thy mother various and wavering; from the loins of thy father inheritest thou instability: how then shalt thou be firm?

Those who gave thee a body furnished it with weakness; but he who gave thee a soul, armed thee with resolution: employ it and thou art wise: be wise and thou art happy.

Let him who doeth well, beware how he boasteth of it: for rarely is it of his own will.

Is it not the event of an impulse from without? born of uncertainty; enforced

enforced by accident; dependent on somewhat else? to these then, and to accident is the praise due.

Beware of irresolution in the intent of thy actions; beware of instability in the execution; so shalt thou triumph over two great failings of thy nature.

What reproacheth reason more than to act contrarieties? what can suppress the tendencies to these, but firmness of mind?

The Inconstant feeleth that he changeth, but he knoweth not why; he seeth that he escapeth from himself, but he perceiveth not how: be thou incapable of change in that which is right; and men will rely upon thee.

Establish unto thyself principles of action; and see that thou ever act according to them.

First know that thy principles are just; and then be thou inflexible in the path of them.

So shall thy passions have no rule over thee: so shall thy constancy ensure

sure unto thee the good thou possessest; and drive from thy door misfortune: anxiety and disappointment shall be strangers to thy gates.

Suspect not evil in any one, until thou seest it: when thou seest it, forget it not.

Whoso hath been an enemy, cannot be a friend; for man mendeth not of his faults.

How should his actions be right, who hath no rule of life? Nothing can be just which proceedeth not from reason.

The Inconstant hath no peace in his soul; neither can any be at ease, whom he concerneth himself with.

His life is unequal: his motions are irregular: his soul changeth with the weather.

To-day he loveth thee; to-morrow thou art detested by him: and why? Himself knoweth not wherefore he loved, or wherefore he now hateth.

To-day he is the tyrant; to-morrow thy servant is less humble; and why? He who is arrogant without power, will be servile where there is no subjection.

To-day he is profuse; to-morrow he grudgeth unto his mouth that which it should eat: thus it is with him that knoweth not moderation.

Who shall say of the camelion he is black, when the moment after, the verdure of the grass overspreadeth him?

Who shall say of the Inconstant he is joyful, when his next breath shall be spent in sighing?

What is the life of such a man but the phantom of a dream? In the morning he riseth happy; at noon he is on the rack: this hour he is a god; the next below a worm: one moment he laugheth; the next he weepeth: he now willeth; in an instant he willeth not; and in another he knoweth not whether he willeth or no.

Yet neither ease nor pain have fixed themselves on him; neither is he waxed ed greater, or become less; neither hath he had cause for laughter, nor reason for his sorrow: therefore shall none of them abide with him.

The happiness of the Inconstant is as a palace built on the surface of the sand; the blowing of the wind carrieth away its foundation: what wonder then that it falleth?

But what exalted form is this, that hitherward directs its even, its uninterrupted course; whose foot is on the earth, whose head above the clouds?

On his brow sitteth majesty; steadiness is in his port; and in his heart reigneth tranquillity.

Though obstacles appear in the way, he deigneth not to look down upon them: tho' heaven and earth oppose his passage, he proceedeth.

The mountains sink beneath his tread: the waters of the ocean are dried up under the sole of his foot.

The tiger throweth herself across his way in vain; the spots of the leopard glow against him unregarded.

He marcheth through the embattled legions: with his hand he putteth aside the terrors of death.

Storms roar against his shoulders, but are not able to shake them: the thunder bursteth over his head in vain; the lightning serveth but to shew the glories of his countenance.

His name is *Resolution!* he cometh from the utmost part of the earth: he seeth happiness afar off before him; his eye discovereth her temple beyond the limits of the pole.

He walketh up to it; he entereth boldly; and he remaineth there for ever.

Establish thy heart, O man! in that which is right, and then know the greatest of human praise is to be immutable.

CHAP. III.
WEAKNESS.

VAIN and inconstant as thou art, O child of imperfection! how canst thou be but weak? Is not inconstancy connected with frailty? can there be vanity without infirmity? avoid the danger of the one; and thou shalt escape the mischiefs of the other.

Wherein art thou most weak? In that wherein thou seemest most strong: in that wherein most thou gloriest: even in possessing the thing which thou hast; in using the good that is about thee.

Are not thy desires also frail? or knowest thou even what it is thou wouldst wish? When thou hast obtained what most thou soughtest after, behold it contenteth thee not.

Wherefore loseth the pleasure that is before thee its relish? and why appeareth that which is yet to come, the sweeter?

sweeter? because thou art wearied with the good of this, because thou knowest not the evil of that which is not with thee. Know that to be content is to be happy.

Couldst thou chuse for thyself; would thy Creator lay before thee all that thine heart could ask for; would happiness then remain with thee? or would joy dwell always in thy gates?

Alas! thy weakness forbiddeth it! thy infirmity declareth against it. Variety is to thee in the place of pleasure; but that which permanently delighteth, must be permanent.

When it is gone, thou repentest the loss of it; tho' while it was with thee, thou despisedst it.

That which succeedeth it, hath no more pleasure for thee; and thou afterwards quarrelest with thyself for preferring it: behold the only circumstance in which thou errest not.

Is there any thing in which thy weakness appeareth more than in desiring

things

things? it is in the possessing, and in the using them.

Good things often cease to be good in our enjoyment of them; what nature meant to be pure sweets, are sources of bitterness to us: from our delights arise pain: from our joys sorrow.

Be moderate in thy enjoyment; and it shall remain in thy possession: let thy joy be founded on reason; and to its end shall sorrow be a stranger.

The delights of love are ushered in by sighs, and they terminate in languishment and dejection: the object thou burnedst for nauseates with satiety; and no sooner hadst thou possessed it, but thou wert weary of its presence.

Join esteem to thy admiration; unite friendship with thy love: so shalt thou find in the end that content surpasseth raptures; that tranquillity is of more worth than extasy.

God hath given thee no good without its admixture of evil: but he hath
given

given thee also the means of throwing off the evil from it.

As joy is not without its allay of pain, so neither is sorrow without its portion of pleasure. Joy and grief tho' unlike are united: our own choice only can give them to us entire.

Melancholy itself often giveth delight; and the extremity of joy is mingled with tears.

The best things in the hands of a fool may be turned to his destruction: and out of the worst the wise will find the means of good.

So blended is weakness in thy nature, O man! that thou hast not strength either to be good or to be evil entirely: rejoice that thou canst not excel in evil; and let the good that is within thy reach content thee.

The virtues are allotted to various stations: seek not after impossibilities, nor grieve that thou canst not possess them all.

Wouldst thou at once have the liberality of the rich, and the contentment of the poor? or should the wife of thy bosom be despised because she sheweth not the virtues of the widow?

If thy father sink before thee in the divisions of thy country, can at once thy justice destroy him, and thy duty save his life?

If thou behold thy brother in the agonies of a slow death, is it not mercy to put a period to his life? and is it not also death to be his murderer?

Truth is but one; thy doubts are of thine own raising: he who made virtues what they are, planted also in thee a knowledge of their pre-eminence: inform thy soul, and act as that dictates to thee; and the end shall be always right.

CHAP.

CHAP. IV.

Of the INSUFFICIENCY of KNOWLEDGE.

IF there is any thing lovely; if there is any thing desirable; if there is any thing within the reach of man that is worthy of praise, is it not Knowledge? and yet who is it that attaineth unto it?

The statesman proclaimeth that he hath it: the ruler of the people claimeth the praise of it: but findeth the subject that he possesseth it?

Evil is not requisite to man; neither can vice be necessary to be tolerated: yet how many evils are permitted by the connivance of the laws? how many crimes committed by the decrees of the council?

But be wise, O ruler! and learn, O thou that art to command the nations! one crime authorised by thee is worse than the escape of ten from punishment.

When thy people are numerous; when thy sons increase about thy table, sendest thou them not out to slay the innocent; and to fall before the sword of him whom they have not offended?

If the object of thy desires demandeth the lives of a thousand, sayest thou not, I will have it? surely thou forgetest that he who created thee, created also these; and that their blood is as rich as thine.

Sayest thou that justice cannot be executed without wrong? surely thine own words condemn thee.

Thou who flatterest with false hopes the criminal, that he may confess his guilt: art thou not unto him a criminal? or is thy guilt the less because he cannot punish it?

When thou commandest to the torture him who is but suspected of ill;

darest thou to remember, that thou mayst rack the innocent?

Is thy purpose answered by the event? is thy soul satisfied with his confession? pain will enforce him to say what is not, as easy as what is; and anguish hath caused innocence to accuse herself.

That thou mayst not kill him without cause, thou dost worse than kill him: that thou mayst prove whether he be guilty, thou destroyest him innocent.

O blindness to all truth! O insufficiency of the wisdom of the wise! know when thy Judge shall bid thee account for this; then shalt thou wish ten thousand guilty to have gone free, rather than one innocent to stand forth against thee.

Insufficient as thou art to the maintenance of justice, how shalt thou arrive at the knowledge of truth? how shalt thou ascend to the footstep of her throne?

As the owl is blinded by the radiance of the sun, so shall the bright countenance of truth dazzle thee in thy approaches.

If thou wouldst mount up into her throne, first bow thyself at her footstool: if thou wouldst arrive at the knowledge of her, first inform thyself of thine own ignorance.

More worth is she than pearls, therefore seek her carefully; the emerald, and the sapphire, and the ruby, are as dirt beneath her feet; therefore pursue her manfully.

The way to her is labour; attention is the pilot that must conduct thee into her ports: but weary not in the way; for when thou art arrived at her, the toil shall be to thee for pleasure.

Say not unto thyself, behold truth breedeth hatred, and I will avoid it: dissimulation raiseth friends, and I will follow it: are not the enemies made by truth better than the friends obtained by flattery?

Naturally doth man defire the truth, yet when it is before him, he will not apprehend it: and if it force itfelf upon him, is he not offended at it?

The fault is not in truth, for that is amiable: but the weaknefs of man beareth not its fplendor.

Would'ſt thou fee thine infufficiency more plainly; view thyfelf at thy devotions! To what end was religion inftituted, but to teach thee thine infirmities; to remind thee of thy weaknefs; to fhew thee that from heaven alone thou art to hope for good?

Doth it not remind thee that thou art duſt? doth it not tell thee that thou art aſhes? And behold repentance: is it not built on frailty?

When thou giveft an oath; when thou fweareft thou wilt not deceive; behold it fpreadeth fhame upon thy face, and upon the face of him that receiveth it: learn to be juſt, and repentance may be forgotten: learn to be honeft, and oaths are unneceſſary.

The

The shorter follies are the better: say not therefore to thyself, I will not play the fool by halves.

He that heareth his own faults with patience, shall reprove another with boldness.

He that giveth a denial with reason, shall suffer a repulse with moderation.

If thou art suspected, answer with freedom: whom should suspicion affright except the guilty?

The tender of heart is turned from his purpose by supplications; the proud is rendered more obstinate by entreaty: the sense of thine insufficiency commandeth thee to hear; but to be just thou must hear without thy passions.

CHAP. V.
MISERY.

FEEBLE and insufficient as thou art, O man! in good; frail and inconstant as thou art in pleasure; yet is there a thing in which thou art strong and unshaken: its name is Misery.

It is the character of thy being; the prerogative of thy nature: in thy breast alone it resideth; without thee there is nothing of it: and behold, what is its source, but thine own passions?

He who gave thee these, gave thee also reason to subdue them; exert it, and thou shalt trample them under thy feet.

Thine entrance into the world, is it not shameful? thy destruction, is it not glorious? lo! men adorn the instruments of death with gold and gems, and wear them above their garments.

He who begetteth a man hideth his face; but he who killeth a thousand is honoured.

Know thou notwithstanding that in this is error: custom cannot alter the nature of truth; neither can the opinion of man destroy justice: the glory and the shame are misplaced.

There is but one way for man to be produced: there are a thousand by which he may be destroyed.

There is no praise or honour to him who giveth being to another; but triumphs and empire are the rewards of murder.

Yet he who hath many children hath as many blessings: and he who hath taken away the life of another, shall not enjoy his own.

While the savage curseth the birth of his son, and blesseth the death of his father, doth he not call himself a monster?

Enough of evil is allotted unto man; but he maketh it more while he lamenteth it.

The greatest of all human ills is sorrow: too much of this thou art born unto;

unto; add not unto it by thine own perverseness.

Grief is natural to thee, and is always about thee; pleasure is a stranger, and visiteth thee but at times: use well thy reason, and sorrow shall be cast behind thee: be prudent, and the visits of joy shall remain long with thee.

Every part of thy frame is capable of sorrow: but few and narrow are the paths that lead to delight.

Pleasures can be admitted only simply; but pains rush in a thousand at a time.

As the blaze of straw fadeth as soon as it is kindled; so passeth away the brightness of joy, and thou knowest not what is become of it.

Sorrow is frequent; pleasure is rare: pain cometh of itself; delight must be purchased: grief is unmixed; but joy wanteth not its allay of bitterness.

As the soundest health is less perceived than the lightest malady, so the highest

highest joy touches us less deep, than the smallest sorrow.

We are in love with anguish; we often fly from pleasure: when we purchase it, costeth it not more than it is worth?

Reflection is the business of man: a sense of his state is his first duty: but who remembereth himself in joy? is it not In mercy then that sorrow is allotted unto us?

Man foreseeth the evil that is to come: he remembereth it when it is past; he considereth not that the thought of affliction woundeth deeper than the affliction itself: think not of thy pain but when it is upon thee, and thou shalt avoid what most would hurt thee.

He who weepeth before he needeth, weepeth more than he needeth; and why? but that he loveth weeping.

The stag weepeth not till the spear is lifted up against him; nor do the tears of the beaver fall till the hound is ready to seize him: man anticipateth death

death by the apprehension of it; and the fear is greater misery, than the event itself.

Be always prepared to give an account of thine actions, and the best death is that which is the least premeditated.

CHAP. VI.

Of JUDGMENT.

THE greatest bounties given to man are judgment and will: happy is he who misapplieth them not.

As the torrent that rolleth down the mountains, destroyeth all that is borne away by it; so doth common opinion overwhelm reason, in him who submitteth to it, without saying, what is thy foundation?

See that what thou receivest as truth be not the shadow of it: what thou acknowledgest as convincing is often but plausible: be firm; be constant; determine for thyself; so shalt thou be answerable only for thine own weakness.

Say not that the event proveth the wisdom of the action: remember man is not above the reach of accidents.

Condemn not the judgment of another, because it differeth from thine own: may not even both be in an error?

When thou esteemeth a man for his titles, and contemnest the stranger because he wanteth them; judgest thou not of the camel by his bridle?

Think not thou art revenged of thine enemy when thou slayest him: thou puttest him beyond thy reach; thou givest him quiet; and thou takest from thyself all means of hurting him.

Was thy mother incontinent, and grieveth it thee to be told of it? is frailty in thy wife, and art thou pained at the reproach of it? he who despiseth thee for it, condemneth himself: art thou answerable for the vices of another?

Disregard not a jewel because thou possessest it: neither enhance thou the value of a thing because it is another's: possession to the wise addeth to the price of it.

Honour not thy wife the less because she is in thy power: and despise him that hath said, wouldst thou love her less? marry her! What hath put her into thy power, but her confidence in thy virtue? shouldst thou love her less for being more obliged to her?

If thou wert just in thy courtship of her; tho' thou neglectest her while thou hast her, yet shall her loss be bitter to thy soul.

He who thinketh another best only because he possesseth her; if he be not wiser than thee, at least he is more happy.

Weigh not the loss thy friend hath suffered by the tears he sheddeth; the greatest griefs are oft above these expressions of them.

Esteem not an action because it is done with noise and pomp: the noblest soul is that which doth great things, and is not moved in the doing them.

Fame astonisheth the ear of him who heareth it; but tranquillity rejoiceth the heart that is possessed of it.

Attribute not the good actions of another to bad causes; thou canst not know his heart; but the world will know by this that thine is full of envy.

There is not in hypocrisy more vice than folly: to be honest is as easy as to seem so.

Be more ready to acknowledge a benefit, than to revenge an injury: so shalt thou have more benefits than injuries done unto thee.

Be more ready to love than to hate; so shalt thou be loved by more than hate thee.

Be willing to commend, and be slow to censure; so shall praise be upon thy virtues, and the eye of enmity shall be blind to thy imperfections.

When

When thou doſt good, do it becauſe it is good; not becauſe men eſteem it: when thou avoideſt evil, fly it becauſe it is evil; not becauſe men ſpeak againſt it: be honeſt for love of honeſty, and thou ſhalt be uniformly ſo: he that doth it without principle is wavering.

Wiſh rather to reprove by the wiſe, than to be applauded by him who hath no underſtanding: when they tell thee of a fault, they ſuppoſe thou canſt improve; the other when he praiſeth thee thinketh thee like unto himſelf.

Accept not an office for which thou art not qualified; leſt he who knoweth more of it deſpiſe thee.

Inſtruct not another in that wherein thyſelf art ignorant; when he ſeeth it, he will upbraid thee.

Expect not a friendſhip with him who hath injured thee: he who ſuffereth the wrong may forgive it; but he who doeth it, it never will be well with him.

Lay not too great obligations on him thou wiſheſt to be thy friend; behold!

the sense of them will drive him from thee: a little benefit alienateth friendship; a great one maketh an enemy.

Nevertheless ingratitude is not in the nature of man: neither is his anger irreconcileable: he hateth to be put in mind of a debt he cannot pay: 'he is ashamed in the presence of him whom he hath injured.'

Repine not at the good of a stranger; neither rejoice thou in the evil that befalleth thine enemy: wishest thou that others should do thus by thee?

Wouldst thou enjoy the good-will of all men; let thine own benevolence be universal. If thou obtainest it not by this, no other means could give it thee: and know, tho' thou hast it not, thou hast the greater pleasure of having merited it.

CHAP. VII.
PRESUMPTION.

PRIDE and meanness seem incompatible; but man reconcileth contrarieties: he is at once the most miserable and the most arrogant of all creatures.

Presumption is the bane of reason; it is the nurse of error: yet is it congenial with reason in us.

Who is there that judgeth not either too highly of himself, or thinketh too meanly of others?

Our Creator himself escapeth not our presumption: how then shall we be safe from one another?

What is the origin of superstition? and whence ariseth false worship? from our presuming to reason about what is above our reach; to comprehend what is incomprehensible.

Limited and weak as our understandings are, we employ not even their little forces as we ought: we soar not high enough in our approaches to God's greatness; we give not wing enough to our ideas, when we enter into the adoration of divinity.

Man who fears to breathe a whisper against his earthly sovereign, trembles not to arraign the dispensations of his God: he forgetteth his majesty, and re-judgeth his judgments.

He who dareth not repeat the name of his prince without honour, yet blusheth not to call that of his Creator to be witness to a lye.

He who would hear the sentence of the magistrate with silence, yet dareth to plead with the Eternal: he attempteth to sooth him with intreaties; to flatter him with promises; to agree with him upon conditions; nay to brave and murmur at him if his request is not granted.

Why art thou unpunished, O man! in thy impiety, but that this is not thy day of retribution?

Be not like unto those who fight with the thunder, nor dare thou to deny thy Creator thy prayers because he chastiseth thee: thy madness is on thine own head in this: thy impiety hurteth no one but thyself.

Why boasteth man that he is the favourite of his Maker; yet neglecteth to pay his thanks, his adorations for it? how suiteth such a life with a belief so haughty?

Man, who is truly but a mote in the wide expanse, believeth the whole earth and heaven created for him: he thinketh the whole frame of nature hath interest in his well-being.

As the fool, while the images tremble on the bosom of the water, thinketh that trees, towns, and the wide horizon are dancing to do him pleasure, so man while nature performs her destined course, believes that all her motions are but to entertain his eye.

While he courts the rays of the sun to warm him, he supposeth it made only to be of use to him: while he traceth the moon in her mighty path, he believeth she was created to do him pleasure.

Fool to thine own pride! be humble! know thou art not the cause why the world holdeth its course: for thee are not made the vicissitudes of summer and winter.

No change would follow if thy whole race existed not: thou art but one among millions that are blessed in it.

Exalt not thyself to the heavens, for lo the angels are above thee: nor disdain thy fellow-inhabitants of the earth, for that they are beneath thee: are they not the work of the same hand?

Thou who art happy by the mercy of thy Creator, how darest thou in wantonness put others of his creatures to torture? beware that it return not upon thee.

Serve they not all the same universal Master with thee? hath he not appointed unto each its laws? hath he not care of their preservation? and darest thou to infringe it?

Set not thy judgment above that of all the earth: neither condemn as falshood what agreeth not with thine own apprehension: who gave thee the power of determining for others: or who took from the world the right of choice?

How many things have been rejected which now are received as truths? how many now received as truths shall in their turn be despised? of what then can man be certain?

Do the good that thou knowest, and happiness shall be unto thee: virtue is more thy business here than wisdom.

Truth and falshood, have they not the same appearance in what we understand not? what then but our presumption can determine between them?

We easily believe what is above our comprehension; or we are proud to pretend it, that we may appear to have understanding: is not this folly and arrogance?

Who is it that affirms most boldly? who is it that holds his opinion most obstinately? even he who hath most ignorance; for he also hath most pride.

Every man when he layeth hold of an opinion desireth to remain in it; but most of all he who hath most presumption: he contenteth not himself to betray his own soul into it, but he will impose it on others to believe in it also.

Say not that truth is established by years, or that in a multitude of believers there is certainty.

One human proposition hath as much authority as another, if reason maketh not the difference.

BOOK

BOOK III.

Of the AFFECTIONS *of* MAN, *which are hurtful to himself and others.*

CHAP. I.
COVETOUSNESS.

RICHES are not worthy a strong attention: an earnest care of obtaining them is therefore unjustifiable.

The desire of what man calleth good, the joy he taketh in possessing it, is grounded only in opinion: take not up that from the vulgar; examine the worth of things thyself, and thou shalt not be covetous.

An immoderate desire of riches is a poison lodged in the soul; it contaminates and destroys every thing that was good in it; it is no sooner rooted there, than all virtue, all honesty, all natural affection fly before the face of it.

The covetous would sell his children for gold: his parents might die ere he would open his coffer: nay, he considereth not himself in respect of it: in the search of happiness he maketh himself unhappy.

As the man who selleth his house to purchase ornaments for the embellishment of it; even so is he who giveth up peace in the search of riches, in hope he may be happy in enjoying them.

Where covetousness reigneth, know that the soul is poor. Whoso accounteth not riches the principal good of man, will not throw away all other goods in the pursuit of them.

Whoso feareth not poverty as the greatest evil of his nature, will not purchase to himself all other evils in the avoiding of it.

Thou fool, is not virtue more worth than riches? Is not guilt more base than poverty? Enough for his necessities is in the power of every man: be content with it, and thy happiness shall smile at the sorrows of him who heapeth up more.

Nature hath hid gold beneath the earth, as unworthy to be seen; silver hath she placed where thou tramplest it under thy feet: meaneth she not by this to inform thee, that gold is not worthy thy regard? that silver is beneath thy notice?

Covetousness burieth under the ground millions of wretches: they dig for their hard masters what returneth the injury; what maketh them more miserable than these their slaves.

The earth is barren of good things where she hoardeth up treasure: where gold is in her bowels, there no herb groweth.

As the horse findeth not there his grass, nor the mule his provender; as the fields of corn laugh not on the sides of the hills; as the olive holdeth not forth there her fruits, nor the vine her clusters; even so no good dwelleth in the

the breast of him whose heart broodeth over his treasure.

Riches are servants to the wise; but they are tyrants over the soul of the fool.

The covetous serveth his gold, it serveth not him; he possesseth his wealth as the sick doth a fever; it burneth and tortureth him, and will not quit him until death.

Hath not gold destroyed the virtue of millions? Did it ever add to the goodness of any?

Is it not most abundant with the worst of men? wherefore then shouldst thou desire to be distinguished by possessing it?

Have not the wisest been those who have had least of it? and is not wisdom happiness?

Have not the worst of thy species possessed the greatest portions of it? and hath not their end been miserable?

Poverty wanteth many things; but covetousness denieth itself all.

The covetous can be good to no man: but he is to none so cruel as to himself.

Be industrious to procure gold; and be generous in the disposal of it: man never is so happy as when he giveth happiness unto another.

CHAP. II.
PROFUSION.

IF there be a vice greater than the hoarding up of riches, it is the employing them to useless purposes.

He that prodigally lavisheth that which he hath to spare, robbeth the poor of what nature giveth him a right unto.

He who squandereth away his treasure refuseth the means to do good: he denieth himself the practice of virtues whose reward is in their hand; whose end is no other than his own happiness.

It is more difficult to be well with riches, than to be at ease under the want of them: man governeth himself much easier in poverty than in abundance.

Poverty requireth but one virtue, patience, to support it: the rich, if he have not charity, temperance, prudence, and many more, is guilty.

The poor hath only the good of his own state committed unto him; the rich is entrusted with the welfare of thousands.

He that giveth away his treasure wisely, giveth away his plagues: he that retaineth their increase, heapeth up sorrows.

Refuse not unto the stranger that which he wanteth; deny not unto thy brother even that which thou wantest thyself.

Know there is more delight in being without what thou hast given, than in possessing millions which thou knowest not the use of.

CHAP.

CHAP. III.
REVENGE.

THE root of revenge is in the weakness of the soul: the most abject and timorous are the most addicted to it.

Who torture those they hate, but cowards? who murder those they rob, but women?

The feeling an injury must be previous to the revenging it; but the noble mind disdaineth to say it hurts me.

If the injury is not below thy notice, he that doeth it unto thee, maketh himself so: wouldst thou enter the lists with thine inferior?

Disdain the man who attempteth to wrong thee: contemn him who would give thee disquiet.

In this thou not only preservest thine own peace, but thou inflictest all the punishment of revenge, without stooping to employ it against him.

As the tempest and the thunder affect not the sun or the stars, but spend their fury on stones and trees below; so injuries ascend not to the souls of the great, but waste themselves on such as are those who offer them.

Poorness of spirit will actuate revenge; greatness of soul despiseth the offence; nay, it doth good unto him who intended to have disturbed it.

Why seekest thou vengeance, O man! with what purpose is it that thou pursuest it? thinkest thou to pain thine adversary by it? know that thyself feelest its greatest torment.

Revenge gnaweth the heart of him who is infected with it; while he against whom it is intended remaineth easy.

It is unjust in the anguish it inflicts; therefore nature intended it not for thee: needeth he who is injured, more pain? or ought he to add force to the affliction which another hath cast upon him?

The man who meditateth revenge is not content with the mischief he hath received. He addeth to his anguish the punishment due unto another; while he whom he seeketh to hurt, goeth his way laughing: he maketh himself merry at this addition to his misery.

Revenge is painful in the intent; and it is dangerous in the execution: seldom doth the ax fall where he who lifted it up intended; and lo! he remembereth not that it must recoil against him.

Whilst the revengeful seeketh his enemy's hurt, he oftentimes procureth his own destruction: while he aimeth at one of the eyes of his adversary, lo! he putteth out both his own.

If he attain not his end, he lamenteth it; if he succeed, he repenteth of it. The fear of justice taketh away the peace of his own soul; the care to hide him from it destroyeth that of his friend.

Can the death of thine adversary satiate thy hatred? can the setting him at rest restore thy peace?

Wouldst thou make him sorry for his offence, conquer him and spare him: in death he owneth not thy superiority; nor feeleth he more the power of thy wrath.

In revenge there should be a triumph of the avenger: and he who hath injured him should feel his displeasure; he should suffer pain from it, and should repent him of the cause.

This is the revenge inspired from anger; but that which maketh thee greatest, is contempt.

Murder for an injury ariseth only from cowardice: he who inflicteth it feareth that the enemy may live, and avenge himself.

Death endeth the quarrel; but it restoreth not the reputation: killing is an act of caution, not of courage; it is safe, but it is not honourable.

There is nothing so easy as to revenge an offence; but nothing is so honourable as to pardon it.

The greatest victory man can obtain is over himself: he that disdaineth to feel an injury retorteth it upon him who offereth it.

When thou meditatest revenge, thou confessest that thou feelest the wrong: when thou complainest, thou acknowledgest thyself hurt by it: meanest thou to add this triumph to the pride of thine enemy?

That cannot be an injury which is not felt: how then can he who despiseth it revenge it?

If thou think it dishonourable to bear an offence, more is in thy power; thou mayest conquer it.

Good offices will make a man ashamed to be thine enemy. Greatness of soul will terrify him from the thought of hurting thee.

The greater the wrong, the more glory is in pardoning it; and by how much

much more justifiable would be revenge, by so much the more honour is in clemency.

Hast thou a right to be a judge in thine own cause; to be a party in the act, and yet to pronounce sentence on it? before thou condemnest, let another say it is just.

The revengeful is feared, and therefore he is hated: but he that is endowed with clemency is adored. The praise of his actions remaineth for ever; and the love of the world attendeth him.

CHAP. IV.

CRUELTY, HATRED, and ENVY.

REVENGE is detestable: what then is cruelty? lo! it possesseth the mischiefs of the other, but it wanteth even the pretence of its provocations.

Men disown it as not of their nature: they are ashamed of it as a stranger

ger to their hearts: do they not call it Inhumanity?

Whence then is her origin? unto what that is human oweth she her exiſtence? Her father is Fear, and behold, Diſmay, is it not her mother?

The hero lifteth his ſword againſt the enemy that reſiſteth; but no ſooner doth he ſubmit than he is ſatisfied.

It is not in honour to trample on the object that feareth; it is not in virtue to inſult what is beneath it: ſubdue the inſolent and ſpare the humble, and thou art at the height of victory.

He who wanteth virtue to arrive at this end; he who hath not courage to aſcend thus into it; lo! he ſupplieth the place of conqueſt by murder, of ſovereignty by ſlaughter.

He who feareth all, ſtriketh at all: why are tyrants cruel, but becauſe they live in terror?

The cur will tear the carcaſe, though he dare not look it in the face while living: but the hound that hunteth it to the death, mangleth it not afterwards.

Civil wars are the most bloody, because those who fight them are cowards. Conspirators are murderers, because in death there is silence: is it not fear that telleth them they may be betrayed?

That thou mayst not be cruel, let thyself too high for hatred: that thou mayst not be inhuman, place thyself above the reach of envy.

Every man may be viewed in two lights: in one he will be troublesome, in the other less offensive: chuse to see him in that in which he least hurteth thee; then shalt thou not do hurt unto him.

What is there that a man may not turn unto his good? in that which offendeth us most, there is more ground for complaint than hatred. Man would be reconciled to him of whom he complaineth: what murdereth he but what he hateth?

If thou art prevented of a benefit, fly not into rage: the loss of thy reason is the want of a greater.

Because thou art robbed of thy cloak, wouldst thou strip thyself of thy coat also?

When thou enviest the man who possesseth honours; when his titles and his greatness raise thy indignation: seek to know whence they came unto him; enquire by what means he was possessed of them; and thine envy will be turned into pity.

If the same fortune were offered unto thee at the same price; be assured, if thou wert wise, thou wouldst refuse it.

What is the pay for titles but flattery? how doth man purchase power but by being a slave to him who giveth it?

Wouldst thou lose thine own liberty to be able to take away that of another? or canst thou envy him who doth so?

Man purchaseth nothing of his superiors but for a price; and that price, is it not more than the value? wouldst thou pervert the customs of the world? would thou have the purchase and the price also?

As thou canst not envy what thou wouldst not accept; disdain this cause of hatred, and drive from thy soul this occasion of the parent of cruelty.

If thou possessest honour, canst thou envy that which is obtained at the expence of it? if thou knowest the value of virtue, pitiest thou not those who have bartered it so meanly?

When thou hast taught thyself to bear the seeming good of men without repining, thou wilt hear of their real happiness with pleasure.

If thou seest good things fall to one who deserveth them, thou wilt rejoice in it: for virtue is happy in the prosperity of the virtuous.

He who rejoiceth in the happiness of another, increaseth by it his own.

CHAP,

CHAP. V.
HEAVINESS of HEART.

THE soul of the chearful forceth a smile upon the face of affliction; but the despondence of the sad, deadeneth even the brightness of joy.

What is the source of sadness but a feebleness of the soul? what giveth it power but the want of spirit? Rouse thyself to the combat, and she quitteth the field before thou strikest.

She is an enemy to thy race; therefore drive her from thy heart: she poisoneth the sweets of thy life; therefore suffer her not to enter thy dwelling.

She raiseth the loss of a straw to the destruction of thy fortune: while she vexeth thy soul about trifles, she robbeth thee of thine attention to the things of consequence; behold, she but prophesieth what she seemeth to relate unto thee.

She spreadeth drowsiness as a veil
over

over thy virtues: she hideth them from those who would honour thee on beholding them: she entangleth and keepeth them down, while she maketh it most necessary for thee to exert them.

Lo! she oppresseth thee with evil; and she tieth down thine hands, when they would throw the load from off thee.

If thou wouldst avoid what is base; if thou wouldst disdain what is cowardly; if thou wouldst drive from thy heart what is unjust, suffer not sadness to lay hold upon it.

Suffer it not to cover itself with the face of piety: let it not deceive thee with a shew of wisdom. Religion payeth honour to thy Maker: let it not be clouded with melancholy: wisdom maketh thee happy: know then that sorrow, in her sight, is as a stranger.

For what should man be sorrowful but for afflictions? why should his heart give up joy, when the causes of it are not removed from him? is not this being miserable for the sake of misery?

As the mourner who looketh sad because he is hired to do so; who weepeth because his tears are paid for; such is the man who suffereth his heart to be sad, not because he suffereth aught, but because he is gloomy.

It is not the occasion that produceth the sorrow; for behold, the same thing shall be to another rejoicing.

Ask men if their sadness maketh things the better; and themselves will confess to thee that it is folly; nay, they will praise him who beareth his ills with patience, who maketh head against misfortune with courage: applause should be followed by imitation.

Sadness is against nature, for it troubleth her motions: lo! it rendereth distasteful whatsoever she hath made amiable.

As the oak falleth before the tempest and raiseth not its head again; so boweth the heart of man to the force of sad-

sadness, and returneth unto its strength no more.

As the snow melteth upon the mountains from the rain that trickleth down their sides, even so is beauty washed from off the cheeks by tears: and neither the one nor the other restoreth itself again for ever.

As the pearl is dissolved by the vinegar, which seemeth at first only to obscure its surface; so is thy happiness, O man! swallowed up by heaviness of heart, though at first it seemeth only to cover it with its shadow.

Behold sadness in the public streets: cast thine eye upon her in the places of resort; doth any look upon her? avoideth she not every one? and doth not every one flee from her presence?

See how she droopeth her head, like the flower whose root is cut asunder: see how she fixeth her eyes upon earth: see how they serve her to no purpose but for weeping.

Is there in her mouth discourse? is there

there in her heart the love of society? is there in her soul, reason? Ask her the cause, and she knoweth it not: enquire the occasion, and behold there is none.

Yet doth her strength fail her: lo! at length she sinketh into the grave; and no one sayeth, what is become of her?

Hast thou understanding, and feest thou not this? hast thou piety, and perceivest thou not thine error?

God created thee in mercy: had he not intended thee to be happy, his beneficence would not have called thee into existence: how darest thou then to fly in the face of his majesty?

While thou art most happy with innocence, thou doest him most honour; and what is thy discontent but murmuring against him?

Created he not all things liable to changes? and darest thou to weep at their changing?

If we know the law of nature, wherefore do we complain of it? if we are ignorant of it, what should we accuse but our blindness to what every moment giveth us proof of?

Know that 'tis not thou that art to give laws to the world: thy part is to submit to them as thou findest them; if they distress thee, thy lamenting it but addeth to thy torment.

Be not deceived with fair pretences, nor suppose that sorrow healeth misfortune: it is a poison under the colour of a remedy: while it pretendeth to draw the arrow from thy breast, lo! it plungeth it into thine heart.

While sadness separateth thee from thy friends, doth it not say thou art unfit for conversation? while it driveth thee into corners, doth it not proclaim that it is ashamed of itself?

It is not in thy nature to meet the arrows of ill fortune unhurt: nor doth reason require it of thee: it is thy duty to bear misfortune like a man; but thou must first also feel it like one.

Tears may drop from thine eyes, tho' virtue falleth not from thine heart: be thou careful only that there is cause, and that they flow not too abundantly.

The greatness of the evil is not to be reckoned from the number of tears shed for it: the greatest griefs are above these testimonies; as the greatest joys are beyond utterance.

What is there that weakeneth the soul like grief? what depresseth it like sadness?

Is the sorrowful prepared for noble enterprizes? or armeth he himself in the cause of virtue?

Subject not thyself to ills, where there are in return no advantages; neither sacrifice thou the means of good unto that which is in itself an evil.

BOOK IV.

Of the Advantages MAN may acquire over his FELLOW-CREATURES.

CHAP. I.

NOBILITY and HONOUR.

NOBILITY resideth not but in the soul; nor is there true honour except in virtue.

The favour of princes may be bought by vice; rank and title may be purchased for money: but these are not true honour.

Crimes cannot exalt a man to real glory; neither can gold make men noble.

When titles are the reward of virtue; when he is set on high who hath served his country; he who bestoweth the honours hath glory, like as he who receiveth them; and the world is benefited thereby.

Wouldst thou wish to be raised, and men know not for what? or wouldst thou that they should say, why is this?

When the virtues of the hero descend to his children, his titles accompany them well: but when he who possesseth them is unlike to him who deserved them; lo! do they not call him degenerate?

Hereditary honour is accounted the most noble; but reason speaketh in the cause of him who hath acquired it.

He who, meritless himself, appealeth to the actions of his ancestors for his greatness, is like the thief who claimeth protection by flying to the pagod.

What good is it to the blind that his parents could see? what benefit is it to the dumb that his grandfather was eloquent? even so what is it to the mean that their predecessors were noble?

A mind disposed to virtue maketh great the possessor of it; and without titles

titles it will raise him above the vulgar.

He will acquire honour while others receive it; and will he not say unto them, such were the men whom thou gloriest in being derived from?

As the shadow waiteth on the substance, even so true honour attendeth upon virtue.

Say not that honour is the child of boldness, nor believe thou that the hazard of life alone can pay the price of it: it is not to the action that it is due, but to the manner of performing it.

All are not called to the guiding the helm of state; neither are armies to be commanded by every one: do well in that which is committed to thy charge, and praise shall remain upon thee.

Say not that difficulties are necessary to be conquered; or that labour and danger must be in the way to renown; the woman who is chaste is she not praised? the man who is honest deserveth he not to be honoured?

The

The thirst of fame is violent; the desire of honour is powerful: and he who gave them to us, gave them for great purposes.

When desperate actions are necessary to the public; when our lives are to be exposed for the good of our country, what can add force to virtue, but ambition?

It is not the receiving honour that delighteth the noble mind: its pride is the deserving it.

Is it not better men should say why hath not this man a statue? than that they should ask why he hath one?

The ambitious will always be first in the croud, he presseth forward, he looketh not behind him: more anguish is it to his soul to see one before him, than joy to leave thousands at a distance.

The root of ambition is in every man, but it riseth not in all: fear keepeth it down in some; in many it is suppressed by modesty.

It is the inner garment of the soul:

182   The OECONOMY   Part II.
the first thing put on by it with the flesh, and the last it layeth down at its separation from it.

It is an honour to thy nature when worthily employed: when thou directest it to wrong purposes, it shameth and destroyeth thee.

In the breast of the traitor ambition is covered: hypocrisy hideth his face under her mantle; and cool dissimulation furnisheth her with smooth words: but in the end men shall see what she is.

The serpent loseth not his sting, tho' benumbed with the frost; the tooth of the viper is not broken, tho' the cold closeth his mouth: take pity on his state and he will shew thee his spirit: warm him in thy bosom, and he will requite thee with death.

He that is truly virtuous, loveth virtue for herself; he disdaineth the applause which ambition aimeth after.

How pitiable were the state of virtue if she could not be happy but from another's another's praise! she is too noble to seek recompence, and no more will, than can be rewarded.

The higher the sun ariseth, the less shadow doth he make: even so the greater is the virtue, the less doth it covet praise: yet cannot it avoid its reward in honours.

Glory, like a shadow, flieth him who pursueth it; but it followeth at the heels of him who would fly from it: if thou courtest it without merit thou shalt never attain unto it: if thou deservest it, though thou hidest thyself, it will never forsake thee.

Pursue that which is honourable, do that which is right; and the applause of thine own conscience will be more joy to thee than the shouts of millions who know not that thou deservest them.

CHAP. II.
SCIENCE and LEARNING.

THE noblest employment of the mind of man is the study of the works of his Creator.

To him whom the science of nature delighteth, every object bringeth a proof of his God: and every thing that proveth this, giveth cause of adoration.

His mind is lifted up to heaven every moment: his life is one continued act of devotion.

Casteth he his eye towards the clouds, findeth he not the heavens full of wonders? looketh he down to the earth, doth not the worm proclaim to him,—Could less than omnipotence have formed me?

While the planets perform their courses: while the sun remaineth in his place: while the comet wandereth through the liquid air, and returneth to its destin'd road again: who but thy God, O man! could have formed them?

what but infinite wisdom could have appointed them their laws?

Behold how awful their splendour! yet do they not diminish: lo! how rapid their motions! yet one runneth not in the way of another.

Look down upon the earth, and see her produce: examine her bowels, and behold what they contain: hath not wisdom and power ordained the whole?

Who biddeth the grass to spring up? who watereth it at its due seasons? behold the ox croppeth it: the horse and the sheep feed they not upon it? who is he that provideth it for them?

Who giveth increase to the corn which thou sowest? and returneth it to thee a thousand fold?

Who ripeneth for thee the olive in its time? and the grape also, tho' thou knowest not the cause of it?

Can the meanest fly create itself? or couldst thou, being aught less than God, —couldst thou have fashioned it?

The beasts feel that they exist; but they

they wonder not at it; they rejoice in their life, but they know not that it shall end: each performeth its course in succession; nor is there a loss of one species in a thousand generations.

Thou who seest the Whole as admirable as its Parts; canst thou better employ thine eye than in tracing out thy Creator's greatness in them; thy mind than in examining their wonders?

Power and mercy are displayed in their formation: justice and goodness shine forth in the provision that is made for them: all are happy in their several ways; nor envieth one the other.

What is the study of words compared with this? wherein is knowledge, but in the study of nature?

When thou hast adored the fabric, enquire into its use: for know the earth produceth nothing but may be of good to thee: are not food and raiment, and the remedies for thy diseases all derived from the earth alone?

Who is wise then but he that knoweth

eth it? who hath underſtanding but he that contemplateth it? for the reſt, whatever ſcience hath moſt utility; whatever knowledge hath leaſt vanity; prefer theſe unto the others; and profit of them for the ſake of thy neighbour!

To live and to die; to command and to obey; to do and to ſuffer; are not theſe all that thou haſt further to care about? morality ſhall teach thee theſe: the œconomy of life ſhall lay them before thee.

Behold they are written in thine heart, and thou needeſt only to be reminded of them: they are eaſy of conception; be attentive, and thou ſhalt retain them.

All other ſciences are vain, all other knowledge is boaſt: lo! it is not neceſſary or beneficial to man, nor doth it make him more good or more honeſt.

Piety to thy God, and benevolence to thy fellow creatures, are they not thy great duties? what ſhall teach thee the one, or what ſhall inform thee of the other, like unto the ſtudy of his works?

BOOK V.
Of Natural ACCIDENTS.

CHAP. I.
PROSPERITY and ADVERSITY.

LET not prosperity elate thine heart above measure: neither let thy soul be depressed unto the grave, because fortune beareth hard against thee.

Her smiles are not stable, therefore build not thy confidence upon them; her frowns endure not for ever, therefore let hope teach thee patience.

To bear adversity well is difficult: but to be temperate in prosperity is the height of wisdom.

Good and ill are the tests by which thou art to know thy constancy; nor is there aught else that can tell thee the powers of thine own soul: be therefore watchful when these are upon thee.

Behold prosperity how sweetly she flattereth thee; how insensibly she robbeth thee of thy strength and thy vigour?

Tho' thou hast been constant in ill fortune; tho' thou hast been invincible in distress; yet by her thou art conquered: not knowing that thy strength returneth not again, and yet that thou again mayst need it.

Affliction moveth our enemies to pity; success and happiness cause even our friends to envy.

Adversity is the seed of well doing! it is the nurse of heroism and boldness: who that hath enough will endanger himself to have more? who that is at ease will set his life on the hazard?

True virtue will act under all circumstances: but men see most of its effects when accidents concur.

In adversity man seeth himself abandoned by others; he findeth that all his hopes are centered within himself: he rouseth his soul; he encountereth his difficulties, and they yield before him.

In prosperity he fancieth himself safe; he thinketh he is beloved of all that smile about his table: he groweth careless and remiss: he seeth not the danger that is before him: he trusteth to others, and in the end they deceive him.

Every man can advise his own soul in distress: but prosperity blindeth the truth.

Better is the sorrow that leadeth to contentment, than the joy that rendereth man unable to endure distress, and afterwards plungeth him into it.

Our passions dictate to us in all our extremes; moderation is the effect of wisdom.

Be upright in thy whole life; be content in all its changes: so shalt thou make thy profit out of all occurrences; so shall every thing that happeneth unto thee be the source of praise.

The wise maketh every thing the means of advantage; and with the same countenance beholdeth he all the faces of fortune: he governeth the good, he conquereth the evil; he is unmoved in all.

Presume not in prosperity, neither despair in adversity: court not dangers, nor meanly fly from before them: dare to despise whatever will not remain with thee.

Let not adversity tear off the wings of hope; neither let prosperity obscure the light of prudence.

He who despaireth of the end, shall never attain unto it; and he who seeth not the pit, shall perish therein.

He who calleth prosperity his good; who hath said unto her, with thee will I establish my happiness: lo! he anchoreth his vessel in a bed of sand, which the return of the tide washeth away.

As the water that passeth from the mountains, kisseth, in its way to the ocean, every field that bordereth the rivers; as it tarrieth not in any place; even so fortune visiteth the sons of men:

men: her motion is inceffant, fhe will not ftay: fhe is unftable as the winds, how then wilt thou hold her? when fhe kiffeth thee thou art bleffed, but behold, as thou turneft to thank her, fhe is gone unto another.

CHAP. II.

PAIN and SICKNESS.

THE ficknefs of the body affecteth even the foul: the one cannot be in health without the other.

Pain is of all ills that which is moft felt; and it is that which from nature hath the feweft remedies.

When thy conftancy faileth thee, call in thy reafon: when thy patience quitteth thee, call in thy hope.

To fuffer is a neceffity entailed upon thy nature; wouldft thou that miracles fhould protect thee from it? or fhalt thou repine becaufe it happeneth unto thee, when lo! it happeneth unto all?

It is injustice to expect exemption from that thou wert born unto: submit with modesty to the laws of thy condition.

Wouldst thou say to the seasons, pass not on, lest I grow old? is it not better to suffer with an equal mind that which thou canst not avoid?

Pain that endureth long is moderate; blush therefore to complain of it: that which is violent is short; behold thou seest the end of it.

Thy body was created to be subservient to the soul: while thou afflictest the soul for pain, behold thou settest the body above it.

As the wise afflicteth not himself because a thorn teareth his garment: so the patient grieveth not his soul because that which covereth it is injured.

CHAP. III.

DEATH.

AS the production of the metal proveth the work of the alchemist: so is death the test of our lives; the assay which sheweth the standard of all our actions.

Wouldst thou judge of a life, examine the period of it: the end crowneth the attempt; and where dissimulation is no more, there truth appeareth.

He hath not spent his life ill, who knoweth to die well; neither can he have lost all his time, who employeth the last portion of it to his honour.

He was not born in vain who dieth as he ought: neither hath he lived unprofitably who dieth happily.

He that considereth he is to die, is content while he liveth: he who striveth to forget it, hath no pleasure in any thing: his joy appeareth to him a jewel which

of Human Life. 195
which he expecteth every moment he shall lose.

Wouldst thou learn to die nobly; let thy vices die before thee. Happy is he who endeth the business of his life before his death; who, when the hour cometh, hath nothing to do but to die; who wisheth not delay, because he hath no longer use for time.

Avoid not death, for it is a weakness; fear it not, for thou understandest not what it is; all that thou certainly knowest is this, that it putteth an end to thy sorrows.

Think not the longest life the happiest! that which is best employed doth man the most honour; himself shall rejoice after death in the advantages of it.

This is the compleat ŒCONOMY of HUMAN LIFE.

THE END.

NEW BOOKS, Printed and Sold by M. LUCKMAN, in Broad-gate, Coventry.

1. A New and neat Edition of Dr. *Watts*'s PSALMS and HYMNS, printed on a fine Writing Paper, and adorned with a Head of the Author. Price 1s. 8d. each.

2. A COLLECTION of HYMNS, from the best Writers; in a great Variety of Measures, adapted to the modern Tunes: Intended as a Supplement to Dr. *Watts*'s, and printed in the same Size. By the Rev. G. *Burder*, of *Coventry*. The 2d Edition. Price 1s. bound.

3. Mrs. *Rowe*'s Devout EXERCISES of the HEART. Small Size. With a Frontispiece. Price 1s. bound.

4. A new and neat Pocket Edition of the DEATH of ABEL. With a Frontispiece. Price 1s. bound.

5. FABLES, by the late Mr. *Gay*; in one Volume complete. Small Size. With a Frontispiece. Price 1s. bound.

6. WISDOM in MINIATURE: Being a Collection of Divine, Moral, and Historical Sentences, selected from the most approved Authors, both ancient and modern; intended principally for the Entertainment and Instruction of Youth. Small Size. With a Frontispiece. Price 1s. bound.

7. Dr. *Watts*'s SONGS for CHILDREN, and Dr. *Doddridge*'s PRINCIPLES of the CHRISTIAN RELIGION, complete. With a Cut to each Song. Small Size. Price 6d.

www.ingramcontent.com/pod-product-compliance
Lightning Source LLC
LaVergne TN
LVHW061213060426
835507LV00016B/1918